Are you impressed?

An exploration of the pressure to perform and impress from the perspective of an organisational development consultant.

Sune Bjørn Larsen
August 2020

Submitted to the University of Hertfordshire in partial fulfilment of the requirements for the degree of doctorate in management

Sune Bjørn Larsen

Are you impressed?

Forlag: BoD – Books on Demand, København, Danmark

Tryk: BoD – Books on Demand, Norderstedt, Tyskland

ISBN: 9788743031741

Abstract

Consultants are under pressure to perform and project an image of themselves as competent and credible within the practice of organisational development. Wanting to create a good impression is inherent in most human interaction and consultants may wish to appear knowledgeable, trustworthy, ethically aware or relaxed because it has an impact on the relation, the task and their sense of self. Being caught up in trying to impress clients and avoid disappointment might have negative implications. It might deflect the consultant's attention from first, the patterns of behaviour in groups and the relational character of organisational development and secondly, from the politics and ethics of the situation. Impression management requires careful ethical consideration because it has consequences for others, and it expresses and influences the sense of self for the consultant as well as for the clients.

I have employed auto-ethnography as a broad methodological approach to describing narratives and reflexively inquire into them. The narratives explore micro-interactions that build, threaten and develop the client-consultant relationship from the perspective of a Danish consultant within organisational development working primarily in the public sector.

In this thesis I incorporate a dramaturgical view on consultancy as a performance where individuals are trying to manage the impression they make on others (Goffman, 1959). Drawing on Elias's processual sociology (1978) and Bourdieu's understanding of power (2005), I argue that the individually experienced need to impress is a pressure in relation to clients. Impressing clients in particular ways is an inevitable part of the politics of consultancy within organisational development. Impression management is entangled with power whereby the consultant always engages in political and moral struggles rather than acts as a neutral helper. The emotional reactions to disappointing or impressing people are related to the pressures created by the political and economic conditions of consultancy.

I suggest that reflexive inquiry creates possibilities for consultants to gain detachment from the pressure to impress as competent, knowledgeable, helpful, and decisive, which might enable them to pay more attention to how politics and ethics work within the role of the consultant. Impression management is relational but is also individual at the same time because it expresses the consultants' identity and ethical position. The thesis proposes Ricoeur's notion of mutual recognition (1992, 2005) as an ethical approach to take others seriously within consultancy in organisational development. Taking clients seriously in the spirit of mutual recognition implies that consultants strive to give an honest account of themselves to take a position and yet listen to others and be open to changing this position at the same time.

Key authors: N. Elias, G.H. Mead, I. Goffman, I. Burkitt, R. Stacey, C. Mowles, P. Bourdieu, P. Ricoeur.

Keywords: Disappointment, impression management, consultancy, organisational development, recognition.

Important note: Names of individuals, organisations, locations, etc. in this thesis have been anonymised.

Acknowledgments

I owe my sincere thanks to the doctor of management research community, particularly to my learning set colleagues: Helle T. Stoltz, Rikke H. Sørensen, Nama Sidi, and Graham Curtis and my supervisors, Emma Crewe and Chris Mowles, for their curiosity, care, and support.

I wish to thank all of my clients for participating in the exploration of my practice as a consultant with them, especially those who have been willing to participate in the narratives. I deeply admire their honesty and courage. I have also drawn on the sharp minds of many friends and colleagues, particularly Christina Levin, Jesper Gregersen, Søren Bjørn Larsen, and Thit Jensen whose help, as fellows in organisational work, has been invaluable.

I am grateful to my family and friends who have participated in and supported my endeavours: my parents for their unconditional love and willingness to engage in the reflexive inquiry with me. Getting to know them and myself is, fortunately, without end. Lastly, I am grateful for my wife Maria Torp Larsen, who has supported me with her love, care, and, not least, patience.

Table of content

Introduction **12**

Project 1: An exploration of recognition and values **17**

My thinking 17

Reflections on my period as a manager 29

From competition to recognition 34

Research question and further inquiry 37

Project 2: Control, affirmation, and emotions **39**

Narrative: Getting the job 40

Control 44

Positive thinking and inflated sense of control 53

Emotions as biology 59

Control, emotions, and relations 68

Project 3: Consultancy and impression management **72**

Narrative: Disappointment in the management group 74

Process Consulting 80

The perspective of complex responsive processes of relating 86

Performing to impress 99

Project 4: Power, identity, and ethics in consultancy **108**

Narrative: My stand as a consultant 110

Doing good as a consultant? 126

Mutual recognition, narrative identity, and identity change 137

Generalising reflections on impression management, power, and ethics in
consultancy 141

Synopsis 147

Method 149

Research ethics 162

Project 1: An exploration of recognition and values 164

Project 2: Control, affirmation, and emotions 168

Project 3: Consultancy and impression management 173

Project 4: Power, identity, and ethics in consultancy 180

Key arguments 185

Argument 1: Consultants experience a need to impress their clients due to a
relational, rather than merely individual, pressure to perform 186

Argument 2: Impressing clients in particular ways is an inevitable part of the
politics of consultancy within organisational development because consultants
are not neutral actors 190

Argument 3: Impressing clients in an ethical way requires self-constancy, taking a
position and yet being open to change this position at the same time 198

Contributions of this thesis 204

Further research 214

References 216

Introduction

This thesis takes issue with a contemporary discussion in the field of organisational development. It has increasingly become the norm to talk about individuals as resources with inner potentials to be unleashed. 'Nowadays, the ideal employees are those who see themselves as reservoirs of competencies, and consider it their own responsibility to monitor, develop and optimise those skills' (Brinkmann, 2017, p. 4). Individuals' self-improvement has dominated the discourse of work for many years (Brinkmann, 2017; Ehrenreich, 2010; Sennett, 1998; Stein, 2017). Brinkmann and many other scholars have problematised how the pressure to self-improve without end is a relatively recent phenomenon in human history that might lead to stress, exhaustion, fatigue and depression (Brinkmann, 2017; Han, 2015; Sennett, 1998, 2007; Taylor, 1991). These critical views have not received broad public attention though. Therefore, it was remarkable that Brinkmann's book *Stand Firm: Resisting the Self-Improvement Craze* (2017) became a bestseller followed by a sold-out lecture-tour in Denmark when it was released in 2014. Taking issue with the ideal of continual self-improvement seemed highly resonant to many.

As a consultant working within organisational development primarily in the public sector I welcomed this as an opportunity to think about how these ideals affect organisational life. Consultants are often described as contributing to the pressure on continual improvement, obsessed with change and pejoratively depicted as 'virtuosos in symbolic manipulation' (Jackall in Clark & Salaman, 1998, p. 22), always ready to reformulate 'problems' to 'challenges' or 'failures' to 'learning potentials'. In contrast, I have found it highly relevant and rewarding when I have managed to explore and discuss failure, disappointment, feelings of incompetence and not being good enough with clients. However, it seems dangerous to admit failure, vulnerabilities and doubt especially in the public space. According to the sociologist Goffman (1959) we all put an effort into managing the impression we make in others to appear competent and failure is far away from the ideal of the competent consultant. Impression management is important to get and keep jobs as a consultant and to help managers and employees with their problems, yet we rarely discuss how we do it, why we do it and how it affects our work within organisational development. But if consultants focus too hard on their appearance rather than being curious together or engaging in creating public good, they might fail to pay attention to power and the ethics involved in the situation. This is displayed in the excerpt below, taken from one of the reflexive narratives that I describe and analyse in this thesis. I was hired by two management groups to work with their strategy but ended up in a power struggle between the managers John and Peter.

> I had facilitated the days as requested, but I felt like a puppet on a string, initially with John as the puppeteer, superseded by Peter. I sympathised with both of them for their dedication to improving the lives of mentally disabled children but felt it had turned into a primitive battle of egos. I could not understand why they were not able to discuss their disagreements in a civilised manner.

I found myself in a fix and unable to act in the situation as a consultant. I was disappointed with them and disappointed with myself for not being able to solve the situation. I feared that they would not think positively about me if I intervened. I realised that being dependent on their positive affirmation as a consultant was part of the power relation between clients and consultants. The nuances and subtleties in which we manage the impression of ourselves as consultants are inherent parts of power games, identity and ethics in organisational life. This led me to refine my research question as follows.

How does the pressure to perform and impress others affect consultancy in organisational development?

As indicated by my title *Are you impressed?* I wish to explore how the presentation of oneself is related to the pressure to impress as a consultant. The title also serves as a reminder for me. So, when I am impressed by others or when I am impressing others (or at least find myself trying to) it is also a call to ask myself: What are we doing and why are we doing it? Stacey phrased these questions as a fundamental approach to researching into organisational life (2012, p. 124). As the point of departure in my inquiry I assume that individuals always leave an impression on others as they interact. So, impressing others is understood as the mere process of interaction between people. In this thesis I explore how consultants face certain expectations towards their ways of impressing others and how they consciously and unconsciously respond to these expectations and try to control the impression they make on others; particularly as the experience of a need to leave a positive impression in clients. Although there is a difference between *leaving an impression* and *leaving a positive impression* this is often conflated (as I have deliberately done in the title of this thesis). These two meanings are clearly differentiated in the Danish language as two different words (respectively *'indtryk'* and *'imponere'*). I have described whether I refer to the first or the latter throughout this thesis. This has led me to explore consultants' need to impress clients with curiosity, how and why they do it and what it might deflect. I am aware of the irony that this thesis is also aiming to impress the reader, but I am stressing that impressing others, in the practice of consultancy as well as in academic work, is certainly not all about impression management, manipulation or persuasion. One might also be impressed by hard work, rigorous argumentation and thoughtful considerations and I am not implying that impressing others is intrinsically ethical or unethical. In this thesis I am making the argument that consultants manage the impression they make in response to power and the politics of organisational life in order to help clients but also to get and keep jobs. The motivation to impress others is complex, many layered and changeable and it is important to understand that impressing and disappointing others is part of the economy of consultancy although it is also about recognition, identity and ethics. Consultants might find themselves caught up in trying to impress others as competent and attractive, which can distract them from operating politically and ethically and thereby, being as useful and helpful as they might be. Before I begin the exploration of the research theme that will lead to these arguments, I will briefly describe my approach to research as a guide for reading this thesis.

Research approach

The Doctor of Management programme (DMan) is a professional doctorate that encourages managers and consultants to take their experience and relationships with others as an object of research. It is a requirement on the DMan programme to describe and inquire into narratives from one's own practice with an auto-ethnographical approach. I have set out and developed my arguments in conversation with relevant literature in different disciplines that has proved relevant to the exploration of the experiences I have encountered. The research theme and the specific methodological approach have not been planned in detail from the outset. My research has been problem driven and I have continuously made decisions about what the next step in my exploration should be and which theories could be helpful to explain and understand my practice. This also means that I have reviewed literature throughout the thesis rather than conducting a conventional literature review and presenting the results in one place. I have described my methodological decisions whenever relevant and I have delved in depth into how this has formed as my methodological approach in the method section in the synopsis.

My approach to research was in part shaped by the structure of the DMan programme. This programme consists of four residential weekends a year, with presentations and discussions about relevant themes, ethics and methodology held within a community of around 25 doctoral students and supervisors. We are further divided into smaller learning sets that consist of four students and a supervisor. In between residentials the learning set has virtual meetings to comment on written work, discuss, help, challenge, disagree and continually be reflexive about each student's work. I find that the pragmatist notion of a 'community of inquiry' describes the collaborative research practice I have conducted (Shields, 2003). The learning set and the wider DMan-community have been vital to explore taken-for-granted assumptions in my practice and I refer to their contribution to my research throughout the thesis.

The thesis is a portfolio that consists of four projects and a synopsis. Following my auto-ethnographic approach my first project is an experiential autobiography (Mowles, 2017, p. 228) where I describe how I have become who I am in relation to others and how this influences my work as a consultant. My individual account is relevant as a starting point in the exploration of the broader context of my theme of research. I critically explore the assumptions that I am making and move from my particular experience to more and more generalisable claims throughout the thesis. This foundation allows me to investigate my practice in a reflexive way in project 2, 3 and 4. These projects have reflexive narratives treated as the empirical data that I explore, share with others, and build on to enhance our understanding more generally of my theme of research. Each project has gone through six to nine iterations in response to the comments, critique and discussions with learning set and supervisors. Once I have finished each project, I have left it untouched to display the emergent character of this research and to demonstrate the development in my thinking and practice. This means that the first project that follows after this introduction was finished nearly two and half years ago. The last project is a synopsis that contains reflexive turns on the projects, description of method, key arguments, research ethics and contribution to knowledge and practice.

Project 1: An exploration of recognition and values

My thinking

In this project, I will explore how I think about my work practice. I will describe significant events, experiences, and periods in my life. I will reflect upon how they have influenced my way of thinking and how my thinking has evolved throughout my childhood, studies, and work experiences. To understand how I think, I will explain a little about values in my family.

Childhood

I was born in 1975 and raised in a small city in Denmark on the edge of the countryside. I have two brothers and a sister. We were closely connected in our family, and we still are. My grandparents on my father's side were farmers and actively involved in the local Christian church society. They started their adult life with a small piece of land without electricity and had been working hard to buy a small farm. My father is a Christian, too, believing in gratitude and giving love to your neighbour. For instance, my parents never locked the front door to our house. I asked my father if he was not afraid that our things would be stolen. He replied that those who would steal our things probably needed them more than us. My father was not a devout Christian, though, and my mother was not Christian at all. We rarely talked about God and Christianity at home, and we went to church only for Christmas. In Denmark, we are taught about Christianity in public schools, and when I was around 14 years old, I had an intuitive sense that God did not exist. I talked about it with my parents, and I remember our talk as a mutual inquiry into beliefs and that they were supportive of how I felt. Later, my sister studied theology and is a priest now. I have enjoyed my frequent discussions with her about Christianity. I see now that my values developed during my childhood as a strong and fixed set of values based on Christianity.

Hard work was a strong value for my father, just as it had been for my grandparents. Towards the end of my primary school, he was a director of finance in the municipality. I was very proud of him, and I wanted to make him proud of me too. I did my best in school, and I got good grades. Sport was important for me too. I used to—and still do—play table tennis. I remember my excitement when telling my father every time I had achieved or won something. I recall the feeling of lying in my bed after a successful tournament. Sensing warmth, feeling recognised, proud, and happy. As the amount of table tennis training increased, it was difficult for me to participate at the highest level and give enough attention to high school at the same time. I had to prioritise how to spend my time. And although I was on the youth national team, I realised I would not be able to be among the best players in the world. So, I decided to slow down on the table tennis career, and I focused more on high school. Good grades in school evoked the same feelings of recognition, and it was important for me to excel in school.

Recognition

When I think back upon these feelings of happiness, I find a strong link between my family valuing hard work and doing my best, which was aimed at getting attention and recognition from my father. I feel this was how I became visible to him. My relationship with my mother was very different. She worked part-time as a librarian to have time for the household and to spend time with my siblings and me. I remember her as available and supportive, and I have always felt recognised and accepted by her no matter what I did. Thinking back, I find it strange that I strived for my father's recognition when my mother's recognition was always there. It was as if I did not find it valuable since I did not have to work hard to get it.

Near the end of high school, I worked as a helper for mentally disabled adult people. I found it important and deeply satisfying to help people who were dependant on help, and I connected this to my Christian values. As high school was coming to an end, I faced the choice of which career path to choose. There was no doubt in my mind that I wanted to go to university. I remember I was asked why and that I could not come up with a reasonable explanation; it just felt like something I should do. I had been serious about my schoolwork in high school, and I had achieved the highest grades in my class. Therefore, I was able to choose whatever studies I liked at university. I applied for psychology and was accepted. In hindsight, I think it was a move that would both satisfy my need to excel and do good for other people.

Psychology and early work experience in the municipality

I started psychology and developed friendships with a group of students who are still close friends of mine. One of them was a student helper in the HR-unit in a municipality, and he recommended me for a job there. In the HR unit, they had organisational development (OD) as a framework, and I got to know the literature in this field (Schein, 1988; French, W. L. & Bell, 1995; Senge, 1990). French and Bell present the framework here:

> Organization development is a planned, systematic process in which applied behavioural science principles and practices are introduced into ongoing organizations toward the goal of increasing individual and organizational effectiveness. The focus is on organizations and making them function better, that is, on total system change. The orientation is on action—achieving desired results as a consequence of planned activities. The target is human and social processes, the human side of organizations (1995, p. 1).

Within the OD perspective, I was particularly intrigued by Argyris's ideas of single- and double-loop learning (Argyris et al., 1985). In summary, the model describes different levels of problem-solving and learning. Single-loop learning is the successful application of experience and known problem-solving strategies to new problems. The problem with single-loop learning, according to Argyris, is that the underlying assumptions are not questioned. If the available experience or problem-solving strategies are not relevant regarding the problem at hand, the problem cannot be solved. Argyris points to double-loop learning instead. This implies a reflection on our own underlying assumptions in order to change these to see our own thinking and limitations and thereby solve the problem. This is not solving the problem in itself but, rather, reframing our thinking. At the time, I understood the OD-perspective and Argyris to mean that although problems can be complex, it is possible to find desired results. It also implied that I could master this as a technique if I worked hard enough. At the university, I gave a student presentation on this subject. The teacher asked me afterwards if I would join him in giving the same presentation at a university class for people from outside the university. I was flattered and prepared the presentation more thoroughly than I had ever prepared anything before. I received positive feedback from the participants, and I felt that I had accomplished something extraordinary. I felt I was recognised as an expert. This triggered feelings of happiness. In hindsight, I believe this has supported my positive feelings towards this particular theory and the underlying idea that problem-solving is an individual competency that brings recognition to me.

During my psychology course, there was a growing interest in social constructionism and the philosophical sources behind it. I delved into this and linked Argyris's ideas about reframing one's thinking to the thinking of Gregory Bateson, Wittgenstein, and Berger and Luckman. I explored the second-order systemic theory from the Milano School and their work in the field of family therapy (Cecchin et al., 1992) and the application into organisational development (Haslebo & Nielsen, 2000). Organisations and individuals are here seen as autonomous systems that we can disturb but cannot control. Language is central as a creator of reality. The sense I made of it was that we can create positive changes for people if we are skilled in our use of language and our second-order thinking. I also interpreted these ideas as a striving for harmony and avoidance of conflict through the use of language.

Appreciative inquiry

I encountered another approach both at the university and at work in the municipality that has influenced me. In my job as a student helper, I was involved in documenting a project called *The Good Municipality*. The project aimed to create a powerful vision. They used the method of appreciative inquiry (AI). AI relies on a social constructionist view and claims that we get more of what we pay attention to (Cooperrider & Srivastva, 1987), so we should focus on what works in order to get more of that. In the process of creating a vision, there was a strictly planned practice for the employees in which only positive things could be discussed. The HR-unit, however, received frequent and persistent opposition towards the project from the staff. Several of the managers felt they were being treated disparagingly and not allowed to speak out. I remember one manager who raised his voice on one of these awaydays. He had recently laid off a group of employees in his department, and he opposed the positive disciplining in angry terms.

I was embarrassed when the critique surfaced, and I was happy that I was only documenting and not on the stage being responsible for the process. I disliked the atmosphere of conflict and critique. I felt the project was a complete failure; I associated conflict with failure at the time, something to be prevented or handled. At the end of the day, the senior consultants and I discussed what had happened. They came up with several ideas. They wondered if it would have helped to put a mailbox by the door, so the participants could have put their negative thoughts in the box on the way out instead of saying them out loud in the room. I remember I thought I would never place myself in a situation where I could be critiqued like that. I wanted to excel and be recognised as a professional within organisational development. On the other hand, I saw that the manager who opposed the positive process was struggling for service to the citizens, and I thought it was disrespectful to force him into this positive thinking if he did not find it helpful. At the time, I felt the dilemma could have been solved if the facilitation had been more skilful. However, due to the study I was doing on my final master thesis at psychology the dilemma was reinforced.

In the thesis, I did research on the implementation of an IT-project in a hospital. I drew on the sociologist Bruno Latour to understand what was happening. Latour argues that scientific facts are constructions that are developed in networks through alliances and negotiations. He claims that we should not have an a priori hypothesis when we try to understand a phenomenon. We should rather see it as connected in networks with the possibility of taking different perspectives. He distinguishes between classical and relativist sociology:

> For classical sociology the actors are *informants*... Relativist sociology has no fixed reference frames, and consequently no metalanguage... For relativist sociology, indeed, everything is grace (Latour, 1996, pp. 199–200 italics in original).

I found that this was a strange and poetic approach to science, but I could relate to relativist sociology as a respectful way to understand the manager who opposed the appreciative inquiry method. Latour made me question the assumptions that I had been taking for granted in the OD-perspective. He made me realise that I had been trying to gain a position where I had metalanguage, while others only had their own language. I did not know how to use these insights in organisational development work though. I was starting to question models and recipes in organisational development in general, but I did not know what to do instead. Without Argyris's model, AI recipes, and other similar concepts, I felt I was just a human with other humans and not in a professional expert position like the one Argyris offered. I have often said that I valued critique both as a consultant and later as a leader. However, when I look back, I do not think I ever did. I was dependant on the positive affirmation and confidence that the expert-role provided to me. In hindsight, I saw the expert position and a human position as opposites.

When I have contributed to a discussion, I strove for recognition. I long for others to respond to me and say it was relevant or clever. For example, at the end of the first residential on the DMan programme, the director, Chris Mowles, said to me that he was glad to have me on the programme and was happy about my contributions. It created an instant bodily feeling of relief and happiness. I felt I was good enough. However, I also felt dependant on his approval, and I am increasingly interested in how this dependency affects how I think. I see a pattern in my behaviour in which I make a great effort to adapt to and excel in order to receive recognition and thereby stand out as a unique and special individual. I am starting to see the striving for recognition as my struggle to exist as an individual. I am also very aware of my referring to things that others have said in order to make them feel recognised.

Work-life

Towards the end of my studies and employment at the municipality, my father quit his job as director of finance. He was 50 years old and, at the time, I had several conversations with him about his decision. He explained that he had experienced increasing symptoms of stress from work. One day, he found his hands were shaking so much that he could not raise a cup of coffee. He did not find it meaningful to work as much as he did, and he felt sorry he had been away from the family so much when my siblings and I were small. So, he quit and started to study again. When he finished his studies, he started to teach part-time. I found this brave of him since it was contrary to ideas of how to excel in a work-life, and it made me happy that he was more present after this.

Meanwhile, I finished my studies and continued my employment at the municipality and later in an HR-unit in a hospital. A few years later, I began working as a self-employed organisational consultant. I was primarily working for the public sector in the social field. I was working with psychological work-environment issues and coaching employees and managers. My business was doing well, and I was proud that I had been able to start my own company. However, at the same time, I experienced a growing dissatisfaction with the content of my consultancy practice. I was caught in the previously mentioned dilemma between the detached systemic perspective and the OD-framework on the one hand and the critical view from Latour on the other. I wanted to excel, but I also wanted to help as a human, and this seemed contradictory. I felt I was part of a game where I had a role to play but that I, from time to time, was not helping my clients. Later, I read what Mowles has written, and I strongly relate to his description:

> Increasingly I felt as though I was expected to be some kind of performer, to distract from what we needed to talk about with a box of tricks, slides containing grids, frameworks and principles to which we could all bend our efforts and find an ideal way of working together (2011, p. 7).

I missed the meaningfulness I had experienced as a helper in social work. I also missed the long-term continuous involvement with and attachment to other people, like I have with friends and family and that I had experienced in my work with mentally disabled people earlier in my life. I wanted to be part of a community and not just slide in and out of organisations briefly entertaining them on my way. So, I applied for a position in a municipality as a manager at a residential institution for children with learning difficulties. I had been doing consultancy work there, and I liked the place and the people. I got the job.

Manager

The job involved lower wages and longer hours. But it allowed me to take greater responsibility and to try to be the manager that I had been advising others to be. I felt I was a participant in an important field of work again. At the age of 32, I was in charge of about 50 employees, and this made me feel like I had achieved something extraordinary. I remember the phone call when I was offered the job. I was driving alone in my car. After the phone call, I parked the car on the side of the road. I checked that no one was looking, and I raised my arms in celebration and shouted, 'YES!' I recall the strong positive bodily reaction even as I write it now— eight years later.

I worked hard to adapt and excel as a manager. I received appreciation and recognition from the managers above, and I was appointed as a deputy for my manager. After three years, her job was vacant, and in 2012, I was appointed as the centre manager for the whole area. This included five large institutions for mentally disabled children including residential units, schools, and other social activities. We were a total of 280 employees. I had excelled, and I was recognised for it with the promotion.

One of the institutions I was a leader for was Enggaard, an institution with about 80 employees where 16 children with developmental disabilities lived. Most of the children did not have verbal language, and they were easily frustrated with resulting violent behaviour. One of the boys was 15 years old and had autism, blindness, and the mental age of a one-year-old. He frequently played with his faeces and was violent towards the staff and his parents. In 2014, the parents of the boy secretly made audio recordings at the institution for three weeks. The relatives handed over more than 700 hours of recordings, and a nationwide morning newspaper published a series of negative stories based on these. The recordings revealed bad language, dark humour, and minor violations of good conduct. As an example, one employee suggested to another, after a night spent cleaning up the boy's faeces several times, that they should put a plug in him (without the boy hearing it and without them doing it). Another example was about a rule that everyone should say their name upon entering the boy's room as he was blind and needed to know who entered. In the recordings, we often heard that the staff did not do this.

The employees were both offended that the recording had intervened in their private sphere but also embarrassed. I found the revelations disturbing, so I made plans, listened to the recordings, and investigated the events we heard on the recordings. The local manager and the employees' union had a significant number of official conversations with staff; we sanctioned everything that differed from the official standards, initiated preventive measures, made new plans, and so on. This process lasted for months and caused insecurity for the staff at the institution, as it was unpredictable what the recordings would uncover and how things would be interpreted. I had never worked as hard as I did or been as worried as I was in that period.

I made plans, worked hard, and tried to do what my superior manager and the politicians wanted. However, unlike earlier in my career, it did not solve the situation. The parents and employees continued to be upset and insecure. The politicians fought over this in public, and some blamed the local leadership. I was misquoted in an interview by a national newspaper, and more inquiries were launched from the municipality. My manager resigned for other reasons, and the higher-ranked director initiated an increasing number of inquiries and requirements for all sorts of documentation at the institution. Although Enggaard had good formal reports and a good internal accreditation before this incident, the trust that the institution had had was replaced by rules and regulations so the higher level of managers at the municipality could cover their backs. My space to manage the work at the institution was increasingly narrowed. The criticism grew, and I found myself with increasing demands, and I was disheartened that my hard work was not enough to solve the situation. Parents with a positive attitude towards the institution, the positive formal reports, and all other positive things slowly moved to the background in the eyes of managers above. The staff began to leave the institution, and recruitment became increasingly difficult. It had been hard to recruit to our area before the crisis, and this was significantly worsened.

A new senior manager was employed. He was a former colleague. On one of the first days of his employment, I had a discussion with him in which he advised me to distance myself from the institution. He suggested that I should let the manager at Enggaard handle the situation and not get too involved since my own involvement would make me responsible too. Just before the Enggaard recordings were revealed, I had been recruited to a talent programme for leaders with the potential to be promoted to the next level of leadership in the municipality. He said that my own involvement could do harm to my position, reputation, and career. I assumed he tried to distance himself from being involved in the crisis and he was suggesting that I do likewise. I think he was insecure in his new position, eager to prove his worth to the director, and trying to protect and help me. I did not, however, find it helpful. I felt he reduced the situation to a matter of personal survival, ignoring the wellbeing of the children and the employees. I found his advice unethical, and I rejected his approach to his face with determination. This is something I rarely do, and it made me uncomfortable, but I found our diverging views on how I should engage and take responsibility as a leader deeply disturbing. I found his statements in conflict with my Christian values. I was not aware of this at the time, but I see that my own values were conflicting too. I wanted to help the children, take care of the employees, work hard, and be loyal as a leader of the centre. I could not see how I could solve the situation in a way in which I would be successful and act in accordance with my values at the same time. His lack of understanding and recognition of my work, combined with my feeling of being unable to help the children, families, and staff I was responsible for, resulted in severe feelings of stress. I experienced physical strain due to the long working days, my constant worrying, impacts on the children at Enggaard and at the four other institutions (because I did not have time to give them much attention), the violation of my values and the lack of positive affirmation. I woke up early in the mornings feeling exhausted, forgetful, and with less patience both at work and home. I suppressed this, explaining it as symptoms in the face of a lot of work and suspected that these symptoms would disappear when the problem was resolved.

The problem and my reactions did not disappear. The crisis had stretched for more than half a year, and I was continuously feeling worse. I suffered from sleeplessness, chest pains, headaches, and nosebleeds. One day, I felt it was all too much. I could not gather my thoughts and my nose had been bleeding several times during meetings. I had desperately been hanging on in order to solve the situation while repressing the symptoms. But on that day, I had to admit to myself that I could not hang on anymore. When I came home that day, I said to my wife that I just could not do the job anymore. She was happy for me. She had seen me fight and suffer and had been worried for a long time. The next day, I quit without a new job, which is a very uncommon thing for me to do. It did not feel as though it was an active choice for me to leave the job. I felt detached from my body and that my body had resigned. I was in a state of shock since I had not been able to control my reactions. In hindsight, I had seen my body as a loyal servant to carry out what I needed, a thing to take care of and a thing my brain could control as if I am my brain but not my body.

Once I resigned, I felt relief that I was not faced with the problems at work anymore. However, I also felt ashamed that I had not been able to solve the situation. Shortly after I had resigned, I was asked about my occupational status at a meeting with parents from the class of one of my children. I answered that I used to be a centre manager in the social area. I immediately noticed how awkward it must have appeared that I replied with my former position. I realised I had found the managerial position prestigious and important to my identity.

Reflections on my period as a manager

Making sense of that now, I see that I had quite fixed ideas about what it meant to solve a situation as a leader. Later I read Mowles' critique of the ideal leader I strived to be:

> So a good leader would be someone who could choose to be transformational, turn things to the positive, decide on change and show themselves to be a leader rather than a manager. In being able to sew all of these things together they will have set out their vision in a coherent and morally convincing, authentic way that demonstrates how they will both inspire and deliver results (2011, p. 92).

I had wanted to be a successful leader in control, able to solve problems according to my values and to receive positive affirmation for my accomplishments. As a part of the talent programme, I had already envisioned a near future where I had moved to the next level of leadership. Instead, I was now without a prestigious managerial position, and I felt like a complete failure. I felt guilty, and I blamed myself for not being able to solve the situation. I also blamed my manager for being cynical with flawed ethics. The lack of positive affirmation clashed with my concerns about the wellbeing of the children, the families, and the employees, and I could not make these ends meet.

Looking back, it seems to me that I had idealised my values as if they were universals and superior to other people's values and seen them without internal contradictions. This makes me curious to understand further the importance of my struggle for recognition and the conflict with values. The German professor of social philosophy Axel Honneth has developed an understanding of the need for recognition that I can relate to. To illustrate this, he refers to the novel *Invisible Man* by Ralph Ellison (Honneth, 2003, pp. 98–99). The novel is about a black man who is treated as if he were invisible in a white society. This social invisibility raises aggression and anger in the main character, and according to Honneth, the book revolves around his struggle to be visible in order to exist. Honneth uses the notion of visibility to show his view on recognition as fundamental in the development of identity. Our identity is deeply social, and we are dependent on recognition. I see that the recognition I have struggled for has primarily been positive affirmation.

Honneth draws on Hegel's dialectic understanding of societal development to explain that what we are recognised for emerges as historically and contextually based patterns (2003, p. 43). Hence recognition at work is strongly linked to our sense of identity. In Enggaard, I felt ashamed that I was not able to be in control and perform. This struggle aroused feelings of stress and panic in me. I see these strong bodily reactions as my struggle to exist as an individual. It rests on the assumption that I can control and solve situations as an autonomous individual. Stacey suggests a different understanding where the individual and the social are not separated: 'Basically, this is a way of thinking in which both mind and society are the patterning activities of human bodies' (2003, p. 2). From this perspective, my struggle was a pattern that evolved in the activities between human bodies and was not located just in me.

Thinking back, I had seen my struggle to adapt and excel as a fixed and unchangeable personality trait that I have inherited from my father. I have even had discussions with my siblings about the pros and cons of this heritage which implies that we have perceived it as a fact. I recognise a similar pattern around my father's struggle as a director. It reminds me of how my own three children who are now aged 8, 10, and 12 still mention that I was rarely home during my period as a manager. When I was home, I was mentally absent or frequently on the phone. They say they are happy that I do not have that job anymore. I see now that I have used my father to explain my own actions. For example, why I wanted to win at table tennis, study at the university, and excel as centre manager; as if my father has been the cause for how I act in my life and particularly at Enggaard. In hindsight, I think he was aware of this pattern and did his best to accept me as a human. I find it unfair to him that I have unconsciously blamed him for my actions, and I find my thinking surprisingly rigid since I had reproduced a pattern that is similar to his despite the conversations we had when he left his job.

Self-employed consultant—again

After Enggaard, I picked up my trade as a self-employed consultant again and tried to recover. I was eager to make sense of what had happened. I had come across the writings of Ralph Stacey and the perspective of complex responsive processes of relating earlier, and I believed I could be inspired to a greater understanding within this theoretical frame. I was intrigued by his argument that responses from others make it impossible to control organisations and that we should rather accept that organisational development is non-linear and unpredictable. I wanted to understand this further and planned to write a book about it with a colleague. We did what many management book-writers have done and found leaders who had been able to handle situations that I had not been able to. We interviewed these managers to get material for the book, to develop our thinking, and to inspire others. We identified the participating leaders' abilities, and we coined them complexity-competencies. We identified four of these: acceptance, participation, reflexivity, and responsiveness (Larsen & Gregersen, 2017). The writing of this project at the DMan has made me see my book in a new light. I see highlighting of leader's masteries as a step down the road of individualistic and linear thinking. I was almost embarrassed when, after the publication of our book, I read the following quote:

> When one makes sense of experience from the strategic choice perspective the most widespread response to the unexpected takes the form of some kind of blame. The response is then to put more

effort into gathering and analysing information to overcome ignorance. Or more intensive efforts are made to acquire the necessary competences to manage strategically and so avoid accusations and feelings of incompetence (Stacey & Mowles, 2016, p.96).

In hindsight, I was still thinking about development as an individual matter. The events at Enggaard made a great impact on me, and I have struggled to make sense of it since. It triggered reflections on several lifelong themes about positive affirmation, universal values, and harmony. I have come to see that I have been trying to control what is uncontrollable, and I have been unable to accept this. I realise I am still rooted in both individualistic and linear thinking as a way to control, perform, impose my values on others, and be recognised as an individual. However, I also find other aspects of our book that did not reproduce my thinking about organisational development. For instance, we invited our network to discuss and contribute to the making of it, and we engaged with their critique and ideas, which made the process very unpredictable. This changed the book substantially from our original ideas, and we were willing to engage with this loss of control. Also, several artists and actors joined the process, and they questioned our way of working on complexity by relying entirely on the use of language rather than other media of expression. This led us to develop and incorporate paintings to express ideas in the book. This challenged my assumptions about how neutral experts cannot use arts, aesthetics, and personal experiences in their work. I see that I have put a great effort into separating this from my work in organisations earlier.

My need for recognition appears in another important part of my life—music and songwriting. I have been playing and writing music for most of my life. However, after my period as a manager, I found relief in writing and playing music as an activity specifically because I enjoyed it and not in order to be excellent. The music I play is in the genre of quiet singer-songwriter music with Danish lyrics. Occasionally, I play with a group of friends at small venues, and I published an album just before I started the DMan. I find that the following quote from one of my songs shows my struggle for identity clearly:

Say my name and I'll say yours—and real is how I feel
Say my name and I'll say yours—and happy is how I feel (Bjørn, 2017).

My musical exertions might seem like another way to adapt and excel, although I deliberately try to keep my focus on the joy of writing and playing music and engaging with the band and the audience. But obviously, I cannot separate the factors of my motivation. Due to my assumption that work and personal life can and should be separated, my writing about music and childhood experiences in this project is highly challenging for me. It still makes me think that I am unprofessional and unserious about my work, and I am afraid how others will interpret this.

In my current work, I am aware of this separation, and I try to understand it further. For instance, I have several groups of employees and managers whom I supervise. There are several common methods that address how to supervise within second-order systemic theory, and I have used these earlier. But I have begun to regard supervision more as everyday conversations about work where we determine what to discuss and how to work together instead of using fixed methods. Also, I see my role more as an experienced participant in the conversation with momentary leadership that is negotiated in the group. I might be judged unprofessional, but I am increasingly prepared to encounter the uncertainty of their interpretation. At Enggaard, I could not control others' interpretation even though I tried. Instead, I see that my assumptions about being a neutral expert prevent intimacy and might cause isolation. I wish to explore this further.

From competition to recognition

Earlier in my life, I thought winning was a personality trait I had inherited from my father. I do have a history of competition, particularly in sports. However, I have also seen my academic career partly as a competition with myself as some sort of a cognitive athlete. And even as I started this DMan, I must admit I have had strategies to plan my way through the whole programme. I have been thinking about whether I should work up a compelling narrative and gradually reveal bits and pieces to form a plausible plot at the very end in order for me to produce a coherent and compelling thesis. I contemplated that 'competition' should be the theme for this thesis. Boiling my thoughts down to 'competition' would allow me to do the academic analysis that I have been successful with so far. Furthermore, having chosen 'competition' as a theme, I made the narratives and analysis in previous versions of this project fit with the concept. But in the process of writing this project, I realised that this reveals how I think, and I am increasingly aware of how the driving force for me was my aspiration to adapt and excel to be recognised as an individual. This made me curious to understand further how my thinking has been influenced in this direction since my childhood. It was also important for me that my parents felt they were represented fairly in this project since I appreciate their parenthood and feel that they have done their best as parents. I decided to send a draft of this project to my parents, so we could discuss the content.

When we met, they had been discussing it between them. They told me they could strongly relate to the description and that it had made them reflect on their parenthood and my childhood. My mother expressed that justice was more important for me than described and that I was preoccupied with what was right and wrong from a young age. My father strongly recognised the issues of control, recognition from prestigious positions, doing one's best, and a sense of justice from his own life. He was happy to read my reflections about values and about doing my best, and he was glad to pass these values on to me as his son. But—like me—he felt it had had high costs emotionally and personally, and he was sorry for the suffering this had resulted in. I enjoyed the conversation with my parents and the common reflection on our family-life, what we have thought and acted, and how this has influenced all of us. My father's reaction confirmed that he ascribes universal status to the values I have been writing about. The whole conversation has increased my awareness of how my thinking has been influenced by others, and it has brought awareness to the responsibility that comes with the influence we have on others.

I was a bit anxious about discussing it with them. I was afraid they felt I devalued their efforts as parents. I realised I wanted to protect them and that I often express the value to do good as a need for harmony and to be nice to others. I see that I have thought of my value of doing good to others as synonymous with being nice. I need positive affirmation, and I try to give it to others. I see how this also influenced how I acted in Enggaard as the conflict with my superior manager was uncomfortable for me. I probably resigned to avoid conflict. I will end this project by reflecting on how my thinking has been formed throughout my life.

My thinking

I have a strong need for positive affirmation, and social acceptance, recognition, and inclusion have given me strong bodily reactions of happiness. I have a strong urge to adapt, control, and excel in order to be recognised and stand out as an individual. I have striven to be an expert in control within almost everything I have done. I have also developed a commitment to Christian values about being nice and avoiding conflict. I have found support for these values in OD, AI, and systemic theory. At times, the struggle for positive affirmation and my values has been conflicting and has exposed me to individual feelings of failure and shame.

The feedback I have gotten on this project has gradually made me see competition to be important only as a symptom of my need rather than a cause that explains my thinking. The opposite of winning for me has been to lose control, to find myself in conflict and perceived as incompetent. It has made me reflect upon alternative approaches in my current work as a consultant. This has amplified the ideas from Latour that have puzzled me since my studies as a psychology student (1996, pp. 199–200). What if I leave the expert position? Of course, my experience with the expert position will always be a part of me, and I am curious to understand how I can participate as an experienced human in interaction with other humans and not as a detached expert through strategic plans, personality profiles, models, and concepts. The recognition that Honneth (2006) addresses, as I understand it, is the recognition as a human being among other human beings. This draws on the belief that participation as a human with another human creates changes in both that you cannot predict or control. I find this stance intriguing, and I am on a path where I pay attention to how my need for positive affirmation affects my thinking and my actions. I wonder how things would have been different if I had not been affected by the lack of positive affirmation the way I was at Enggaard. Would I have engaged further in conflict with my superior manager? Would I have raised my voice on values more stubbornly? Would I have complained to the mayor? In the process of writing this project, I have received comments about how I present myself: that I seem eager to impress the reader, that I seem caring as to how the reader understands and agrees with what I write. In this way, it seems that I not only write about recognition and being nice to others, but I also express it in the way I write. I wish to understand further how my need for positive affirmation affects my work.

I am increasingly critical of the expert position within the OD-perspective and the detached position in the systemic tradition. My interest has turned towards an approach as an experienced human participating in everyday organisational life. But leaving the comfort of OD tools and techniques feels like a loss of control and arouses feelings of anxiety and incompetence. The OD, systemic, and AI approaches might have been a way to maintain an idea of control, to get positive affirmation, and a defence against unpredictability and conflict. But my attempt to be in control as a neutral expert might also distance me from others, cause isolation, and avoid intimacy. I am interested in understanding further how my thinking about the expert position affects my thinking, the thinking of people I work with, and what will happen if I question these assumptions in my work as a consultant.

My thinking about values as something I own has supported that responsibility for failures as well as success was an individual matter and thereby respectively blaming or celebrating myself for both. I am curious to inquire into an understanding of values as a social process and not as universals that are located inside any individual. The conflict between positive affirmation and my values at Enggaard was painful for me. As I mentioned earlier, I see that I have regarded my values as universal and superior, and I was not able to make sense of this at Enggaard. This makes me question values as a set of individually based universal standards. John Dewey has reflected on this and compares it to an almanac:

> The almanac, after all, does not tell the sailor where he is nor how to navigate. It is an aid in his analysis of the required conditions of right navigation (1891, p. 194).

Furthermore, I see that my Christian values about doing good and being nice to others have been strengthened by AI and have been mostly unchanged and unquestioned throughout my life. I find this both worrying and interesting since I want to learn and develop my thinking.

Research question and further inquiry

I will inquire into how my need for positive affirmation and my affirmation of others in order to avoid conflict affects my participation in organisational development. I wish to explore an approach where recognition is based on how we are connected and interdependent as humans and not seen as detached, autonomous individuals. I also wish to explore how values can be understood and how they are part of everyday conversations in organisations.

Project 2: Control, affirmation, and emotions

My reflections in Project 1 brought my attention to my need to be in control as part of seeking positive affirmation but also in order to affirm others. I wish to understand better how control, affirmation, and the relationship between them might be understood in my work as a consultant. Therefore, I will write about my engagement with a new group of people from the initial contact and onwards. I intend to explore control and affirmation as I negotiated the way we worked together. Before I describe what happened, I will provide the context.

In the narrative on which this project is based, I was contacted and asked to supervise a group. Supervision is common in social work in Denmark, and it is part of my practice as a consultant. In my role as a supervisor, I am usually invited to structure meetings where a group of employees are enabled to reflect on and learn from their practice. Usually it is practiced in a group of employees by an external supervisor and without their manager present. The most common supervising method I am hired to work with is called the reflecting team method (Andersen, 1987). This is a way of structuring meetings that is supposed to support reflections and provide help to deal with emotionally challenging events in the work. The method prescribes a set of rules about when and how to talk. Earlier in my career, I was practising this and other approaches that all entail making underlying assumptions about how to control conversations through rules and techniques. However, I have begun to pay attention to how control and affirmation both enable and constrain what happens, and I have been increasingly curious to explore why I experience a pressure to be in control and why the loss of control evokes strong emotions in me.

Narrative: Getting the job

The events in the narrative started with a call from Anna in August 2017. She and her colleagues were looking for a supervisor, and she said she had heard good things about how I supervise. They were family counsellors helping families who faced problems with violence, alcohol abuse, school, and other social problems.

I appreciated that I had been recommended to Anna, but I was also beginning to get too much work, so I decided to turn the job down. She said she was sorry to hear I could not find the time to work with them and emphasised that she had heard I had a critical approach towards strict rules and procedures in my role as a supervisor. She found that this would be relevant for herself and her colleagues. This resonated with my interest, and I was intrigued by her insistence. I felt she had put an effort into the inquiry and that I would disappoint her if I turned her down. So, I agreed to meet. She mentioned that the group had decided to have conversations with another supervisor and me to determine with whom they would prefer to work.

On the day of the meeting, I was expecting to chat to a few people but was taken by Anna to a room with the whole group of 12 people. They presented themselves one at a time formally before I told them about my approach. I tried to convey how the focus of supervision, in my view, is to reflect together on what we are doing and why we are doing it in our everyday work. I explained that I see my role as a supervisor to support these reflections and mentioned that I am often hired to work with the reflecting team method and that I have grown increasingly curious about how this method, and methods in general, allow but also limit reflections. I said that, in my opinion, supervision should also involve discussions about how we work together instead of choosing one method as a default because this might limit reflections in our conversations. Several participants commented that they were happy to work with the reflecting team method. The majority of the group nodded and said they were happy with this method. No one challenged my views directly, but I had a feeling that some disagreed quite strongly with me. I could have asked them if they disagreed and what they disagreed about, but this did not occur to me in the situation. Since I had discussed this with Anna on the phone, I had expected an atmosphere of support, and I was a bit surprised that they were not all in favour of my views. In hindsight, it should not have come as a surprise that among 12 people there would be diverging views, but I realise that in situations like these I usually meet with a few people who are already in favour of my views.

Anna joined the discussion and said she found my views interesting and relevant for the group to explore further. She sat next to a male colleague who supported her verbally. Another colleague sat next to them, and they all nodded in approval with each other. Several others raised their hands and looked at me to participate in the discussion. By raising their hands, they clearly wanted me to guide the order of speakers. I said they could just join the discussion without raising their hands and that, in my experience, a looser structure in supervision, as well as in this current meeting, would allow us to reflect together on how we work together. In that sense, this current meeting was also serving as an example of how we were to work in the supervision sessions. This gave rise to some confusion about who and when they could speak up. People politely looked at each other before they spoke, and some continued to raise their hands. One person asked what a typical session of supervision would look like with me as a supervisor. I replied that, in each group I supervise, we develop our own way of working. But I emphasised that these kinds of patterns are something we need to discuss and negotiate together too.

Since Anna had invited me, I felt I owed it to her to describe my perspective in further detail, so the differences from their usual methods were clear. As I was explaining my views to the group, I noticed how I was trying to convince them that they should choose me as their supervisor. I told them about examples where I had successfully worked with topics that the reflecting team method would not have allowed. While I was talking, I thought that I wanted the job as if it were a competition, and I was curious as to why I was suddenly motivated to get the job.

Towards the end of the meeting, I said that I understood their need to think and discuss who they felt could help them best as a supervisor, and I thought that their reflections on what they needed were important and something they might learn from. Also, the fact that they all attended the meeting, which I had never tried before, showed that they were serious about who they wanted as their supervisor. I think that I left with these messages because I wanted to leave on a positive note to resolve any negative atmosphere due to our differences of opinion.

After the meeting, I felt I had been to a formal job interview. The similarities being that there was more than one candidate, and I was competing to impress those who got to choose. This is unusual since the selection for jobs as supervisor typically does not have a recruitment committee as large and thorough as this. I felt that some were opposing my views, but it was not clear what they disagreed with since they had not brought it into the open and I had not asked them. I had responded to the formal setting and the opposition I experienced with a competitive approach, wanting to perform and get the job. A month later Anna returned with their decision. She said they liked my approach and that their choice had been by the closest margin, but they had decided to hire the other supervisor. I was surprised and disappointed. Immediately, I felt ashamed and that I was not good enough. The kind comments seemed like something she said to soften the blow. This was ambivalent for me since I did need positive affirmation, but I did not want to be pitied. I did not want to appear emotionally affected but tried to control my feelings to appear as if I had simply presented my perspective on supervision and was at ease with their decision. So, I said I was glad they had found themselves a supervisor they felt was right for them. I meant this, but I also wanted to convince her, and perhaps myself, that I was comfortable with their decision. I tried, once again, to end the conversation on a positive note.

Anna had something else she wanted me to think about though. I stretched my patience as she started to explain that their team was facing a merger with another team, and they were searching for a new manager to lead the merged team. In their group, they had discussed what they needed from a manager. During their discussion, the idea of me as their manager had emerged, and she said the group would encourage me to apply for the job. I noticed an emotional shift in me. I had felt ashamed, but suddenly I was honoured that they thought I was good enough to be their manager. I went from a state of shame to a state of pride and confidence. My first impulse was that I would not apply for the job. I was happy with what I was doing so, while we were still on the phone, I thought about how I could turn her down. I felt that I would be rejecting her in an impolite way if I turned her down on the spot. I ended up saying that I would consider the encouragement, and we finished the conversation.

A few weeks later, I received the job post from Anna. It lingered in my mailbox for a week. During the week I stumbled on it several times, and every time I laid eyes on it, I found it silly to be so preoccupied with it. I put an effort into formulating my decision, and I kept thinking that, after all, it was only an encouragement and not a job proposal. It was an encouragement to apply for a job that I did not want, and the odds of getting it might turn out to be the same as the supervisor job. I ended up declining politely, and she replied that she understood my reasons for this. I felt I had finished the correspondence nicely without letting her down, and this made me glad. However, I was also occupied by the nagging thought that I had not told her earlier that I was not interested in the job. I had used a lot of both her and my time, and I had brought myself into a position where I might have applied for a job that I did not want. I have come to the conclusion that my hesitation was because it was important for me that she would not feel rejected.

Initial reflections on the narrative

I chose to write about the detailed interactions in the conversations with this group to understand the subtleties of control as it played out. I felt I was not in control in our negotiations about how we worked together; I could not control the outcome of the events, and I was not in control of my feelings and motivation regarding getting the job. It was as if I was not prepared to take the emotional consequences of rejection, although I deliberately chose to present and advocate for a looser structure that was different from their familiar way of working. Anna and I tried to take care of and not hurt each other's feelings by saying things nicely to each other.

We all tried to maintain a positive atmosphere, but the positive affirmation also made it difficult to understand each other. I sensed that some disagreed quite strongly, but we did not engage in this disagreement. This made me curious about how affirmation might be used to create a positive atmosphere and thereby also used as an attempt to control our own and other's feelings.

This narrative allows me to explore how control is linked to affirmation as we continually negotiate our ways of working in groups. This small and everyday incident contains important elements of control and affirmation as it involves the assessing, judging, rejecting, and promoting of each other in organisations. I set out to explore how I control in order to be affirmed, and my curiosity in this particular narrative was aroused because I was emotionally affected by feelings such as disappointment and shame. This puzzled me, so my animating questions in this project are these: Why is control important to us? What happens when we feel a loss of control? What do we do to stay in control, and how is this linked to affirmation? I will use the narrative to explore and reflect on these animating questions. In the process of exploration, I will draw on relevant theories to understand what happened in order to generalise my claims.

Control

An obvious first step in the understanding of control is to consult a dictionary. The *Oxford English Dictionary* defines control as the power to influence or direct people's behaviour or the course of events. Reed supplements this definition as he describes mainstream understanding of control in organisational work: '"Control" is taken to refer to a co-ordinating mechanism based on asymmetric relations of power and domination in which conflicting instrumental interests and demands are the overriding contextual consideration' (Reed, 2001, p. 201). Streatfield supports Reed's description and adds that mainstream understandings in organisational theory locate control within people as an ability that can move an organisation in a certain direction from the present and into the future (Streatfield, 2001, p. 2). Of course, dictionary definitions and mainstream understandings primarily reveal popular understandings of a word. I was puzzled by the interaction in the narrative because I did not experience that control was only an exercise of power. The power involved in the struggle between interests would be important in the understanding of control, and there are various theories in natural science, politics, psychology, sociology, and organisational theory that describe power in relation to control. I found these perspectives highly relevant, but my interest in the narrative was aroused because I experienced it primarily as an emotional rollercoaster. I found my emotional reactions 'strange, but interesting' (Brinkmann, 2012, p. 12), and according to Brinkmann's view on qualitative research, these strange incidents can direct the focus of our research in everyday life. With control as a theme, I found that my emotional reactions in the detailed interactions revealed a complexity that is not captured in the dictionary or mainstream definitions. It was not only a struggle for control in order to influence or direct other people's behaviour or the course of events but also a struggle to maintain a certain view of myself in my interaction with others that involved emotions. In Brinkmann's perspective on qualitative research, he points to how the exploration of everyday life might make the obvious dubious. As an example of this, I did not experience that I was controlling the events but rather that the events were controlling me. So, who was in control then? I will explore the understanding of control and the links between control and emotions as it played out in the narrative below.

Working with less control

In the negotiation about how we were to work together in the narrative, I presented a looser and, from a mainstream perspective described by Reed and Streatfield, less controlled approach. In my approach, I was inspired by Patricia Shaw (2002) and Ralph Stacey (2003, 2012), and I will describe further how I understand their perspectives. Shaw has compiled the following text from e-mails sent between a group of managers she had worked with to describe what she found important:

This meeting must offer freedom instead of structure, it should have no other purpose than to find out where we are, what needs to be done, what will be our role in future, how do we manage a permanently changing situation. We need to allow meetings which develop their own momentum and results—without driving them into a certain direction. If there is facilitation and a certain structure this must be to help the meeting develop its own dynamic—not to hinder it (2002, p. 16-17).

Shaw describes a perspective where we constantly reflect on what we are doing and why we are doing it together. She describes routines we follow without paying attention to why we are following them (Shaw, 2002). These routines can be seen as stabilising and predictable patterns in our organisational life, maintained because we repeat and confirm them through our daily participation. This concerns everyday relating and communication but also weekly meetings with fixed agendas, strategy meetings, workshops, information meetings, and supervision. This might, however, also hinder our paying attention and listening carefully to each other. Shaw draws our attention to everyday conflicts and to the paradox that continuity and change exist at the same time. In her view, it is important that this paradox is preserved and that consultancy contributes to this and 'amplifies existing sources of difference, friction and contention so that complex learning might occur, provided that people's anxiety in the face of such learning is well enough contained' (1997, p. 241). This resonates with Streatfield's link between control and feelings:

It seems to me that we, as individuals, have a fundamental need to feel 'in control' of situations in which we find ourselves. This need for control is connected to the experience of anxiety, in that the individual need for some sense of control is a way of dealing with the anxiety of not knowing (2001, pp. 7–8).

The loose structure in the meeting and my proposed approach to supervision in the narrative created uncertainty that showed up in several instances: Some expressed openly they were satisfied with the structure that the reflecting team method provided. One person asked about the structure in my way of working with supervision, although I had already explained that this was something we should negotiate together along the way. Several wanted me to control the order of speakers. The reflecting team method provides structure in terms of who can speak and how much they are allowed to speak. In our negotiations about how to work together, I suggested a different structure that was less controlling for the supervision, and I worked in that way in the meeting too. One might argue that neither of us were negotiating but merely presenting our views, but I regard it as a negotiation since our work in the supervision session, if they had chosen me, would have been influenced by how we were relating to each other in our initial meeting.

In our first phone call Anna had told me that the group worked within the framework of second-order systemic thinking[1]. I had not paid much attention to this when she said it, but in hindsight, I think it is important since it holds specific ideas of control that the group was comfortable with. Second-order systemic thinking assumes that we, as consultants, can bring people in a meta-position to their problems (Andersen, 1987; Anderson & Goolishian, 1992; Campbell, 1995; Haslebo, Nielsen, 2000). It also relies on an assumption that systems have an innate pursuit of equilibrium (Watzlawick, Weakland, & Fisch, 1974). The structure in the reflecting team method and the role of the consultant is to control the balance between no disturbance, which, according to Andersen, brings no change to the group, and too much disturbance, which is viewed as conflictual and will, therefore,

---

[1] Besides the reflecting team method, they worked with methods called Signs Of Safety (SOS) and Solution-Focused Therapy among others.

be dismissed by the clients (1987). The structure allows for only certain issues to be discussed and orders who can speak and how things can be uttered. For example, comments to people's cases can be remarked only as curious questions or as appreciative statements. I have grown an interest in how these might also be instruments of control, questioning what these instruments are controlling.

Stacey and Shaw suggest that structures like these serve the purpose of controlling the anxiety and not the outcome, which is somewhat different from mainstream definitions. My experience in the narrative has led me to similar conclusions. My need for control came across as imposing my interests on them because I thought this was right. I entered the encounter with critique about highly structured forms of conversations that relied on systems thinking. I was influenced by how Stacey problematises the idea that systemic thinking separates people as different systems (Stacey, 2003, p. 120) and argues that no one can observe others from the outside as if they are not a part of what is going on. Stacey terms his approach 'the perspective of complex responsive processes of relating'. He inspired my view on supervision in the narrative:

> Supervising and mentoring cannot be reduced to rules, procedures and models… supervision and mentoring are at their most effective in sustaining and enhancing capacities for practical judgment when they take the form of reflexive inquiry into what they and those they are supervising and mentoring are doing together and why they are doing it in the way that they are (2012, p. 108).

He is sceptical of the underlying assumption that anyone can see and analyse a conversation from the outside. I find that the title 'supervisor' misleads one to think that somebody can have super vision. Everybody has vision as participants in the conversation, and as such, everyone influences the conversation, just as the conversation influences us. Of course, we all have formal roles, responsibilities, and expectations of ourselves and each other, which lead to differences in how we can influence what happens. This changes the idea of a supervisor as an instrument to guide and manage reflections to the supervisor as a reflexive participant with a certain responsibility and experience who offers temporary leadership in ongoing conversations (Mowles, 2009, p. 291). My approach in the narrative disturbed their ideas about control. Mowles elaborates on this:

> Whether one is a temporary or more permanent leader in organisations, it is still the case that one is obliged to work with powerful expectations about what a leader should be doing, which both the consultant and the group they are working with play into (ibid, p. 284).

In hindsight, I see that I primarily regarded control as a negotiation that started at the beginning of the meeting. In the light of the events in the narrative, I find that the negotiation had started before we met as we all had expectations towards our work together. With this view, negotiations about how to work together are ongoing with no fixed beginning and end. These expectations of leadership are expressed in seemingly simple processes such as those in turn-taking. An example from the narrative is the practice where people raise their hands to keep a specific order.

> Communicative interaction, therefore, immediately establishes power differences in which some people are 'in' and others are 'out'. The very process of turn taking/turn making, which is the central process of conversation, makes the dynamic of inclusion and exclusion an inevitable and irremovable property of human communicative interaction, quite simply because when one person

takes a turn, others are at that moment excluded from doing so
(Streatfield, 2001, p. 86).

The unfamiliarity with the way of turn-taking I proposed might be linked to
emotions like anxiety. Shaw (1997) argues that it is an important task for
consultants to make it valuable and interesting to explore situations like this. In my
case, I knew that the group was, just like myself, used to working with second-
order systemic thinking, and when I, stubbornly, held on to a different approach,
we were all emotionally affected. One might argue that the situation was too
unfamiliar and uncomfortable for all of us to explore the conflicts that arose when
the leadership of the meeting and the proposed practice in supervision was
altered. In hindsight, I think, for these reasons, I should not have been surprised by
their rejection.

Once I had been rejected, I was ashamed that I could not control whether the
group chose me, and I tried to avoid engaging with the negative feelings it aroused.
I felt that Anna and I said nice things to soothe each other and to avoid negative
feelings. I see this as attempts to control feelings, and in my reflections on the
events, I find that it was blurring the honesty in our communication. Therefore, I
will dwell on why and how we try to avoid negative feelings to stay in control.

Avoiding negative feelings

Working with the narrative has made me aware that the separation of positive and
negative feelings is inherent in everyday relating between people. I have often
heard about and practiced the prescription to start with something positive, then
bring in the negative parts, that should be positively reformulated and point to
possibilities instead of problems, and end on a positive note. This is called the
sandwich model. The technique holds great promises: 'Put together the ingredients
for a feedback sandwich and achievement gains will soar!' (Docheff, 1990, p. 17).
The resemblance between the sandwich model and the message Anna delivered

was striking: First: 'You did really well, and we like your views'. Second: 'You did not get the job'. Third: 'You are good enough to be our manager and you should apply for that position'.

She might not have planned the message according to the model, but in hindsight, I think this contributed to my feeling of 'being handled'. It made me doubt her sincerity: Did they really choose the other supervisor with the closest margin, or did she just say it to be nice to me? Did she encourage me to apply for the position as manager, so I would not feel I had wasted my time coming to the first meeting? In other words: Was her affirmation, at least partly, fake? For my part, I admit that I was partly dishonest on several occasions: when I ended the meeting by affirming them for all being there, and when I said I would consider applying for the position as manager. Due to the reflections on this project, I have noticed that I often end meetings on a positive note as I did both in the meeting and the phone call. The dishonesty is problematic for ethical reasons, and the events in the narrative show that efforts to be responsible through affirming others might also have the opposite effect. We might feel we are being judged by others and handled disparagingly.

According to Fineman (2006) and Clancy et al. (2012), the reluctance to engage in disappointing events and in feelings of shame in organisational life has been amplified by a contemporary 'positive turn' in organisational scholarship. 'Such thinking serves the fantasy of a perpetual sunny side of organisational life where negative emotions can be conquered, eliminated or, worse, managed' (Clancy et al., 2012, p. 527). This was exactly what I experienced in the narrative when both Anna and I tried to manage unwanted emotions and presumed they were not there. I tried to hide that I was disappointed and ashamed, and we both tried to be considerate and responsible towards the other person's feelings. That makes it difficult to engage with criticism. So, we positively affirm others to maintain a positive atmosphere. This might be particularly important to me as an individual, but I also find it to be a wider pattern that covers over a practice where the positive affirmation makes it difficult to understand what the other person means, where we might be outright dishonest or distrust the honesty in the communication because we suspect that others are dishonest when they positively affirm us. My experience in the narrative was that the positive affirmation made the rejection worse because I was insecure about the honesty in Anna's message. I find that this leads to a problem concerning positive thinking. Because, even though Anna might have been genuine, my reaction was to doubt her intentions.

Affirmation was a theme for me in the narrative and also in Project 1 where I mentioned how I was introduced to the practice of appreciative inquiry (AI) during my work at the municipality, and I find that this has influenced my thinking and work in organisational development in general. AI was formulated by Cooperrider and Srivastva (1987) using a radical social constructionist view that 'through our assumptions and choice of method we largely create the world we later discover' (1987, p. 9). With repeated references to the social constructionist Kenneth Gergen, they claim that the positive direction of inquiry will create positive changes in the future. So, the more we focus on something, the more we get of this, and therefore, we should inquire in an appreciative way and not focus on problems. The approach has attracted enormous attention and is commonly used in organisational work (Fineman, 2006), not just as a specific method but also as a way of interacting with each other. In the narrative, we tried to put ourselves and each other in the most positive light. This made it difficult for us to explore disagreements.

Dividing positive and negative emotions

Fitzgerald et al. criticise the practice of AI by saying that it divides the world into contrasting categories, for example, in positive/negative and possibility/problem-contradictions (2010). By exploring only positive experiences, AI 'fails to value the opportunities for positive change from negative experiences, such as embarrassing events, periods of anger, anxiety, fear, or shame' (ibid, p. 223). Fineman elaborates further on the separation of positive and negative emotions (2006) and argues that emotions are 'inextricably welded and mutually informative" (ibid, p. 275). He adds:

> Focusing exclusively on the positive thus represents a one-eyed view of the social world, shielded from the frustrations and sufferings that contribute to the contradictions of emotional satisfaction and their contributions to personal and social development (2006, p. 275).

I found this evident in my narrative, where I reacted with shame upon their rejection and wanted to end the conversation immediately after Anna told me I did not get the job. In their rejection, I experienced that I was not good enough, but in the subsequent encouragement to apply for the position, I suddenly felt that I was good enough. I find that positive thinking supports evaluations and judgment since we experience ourselves as judged about how our performance is to be either positively affirmed or devalued either directly or by a lack of positive affirmation. I could have seen the rejection as a sign of my integrity since I did not compromise over what I thought was right or I could have told Anna that I was sad that I did not get the job. However, I was too disappointed and ashamed to continue the conversation or to explore further into Anna's reflections. By ignoring the painful sides of our interaction, I did not find that it vanished but that it was not dealt with. The result was that I did not explore and learn from what happened together with Anna.

Positive thinking and inflated sense of control

In my narrative, I regarded positive affirmation as an evaluation of how I performed and as a way to support my view of myself. Their rejection was disturbing and anxiety-provoking since it challenged my view of myself as someone who can succeed and get positive affirmation if I put effort into it. Ehrenreich presents a critical view on positive thinking that I find relevant to understanding positive affirmation in a broader historical perspective. Her inquiry into positive thinking started when she was diagnosed with breast cancer (Ehrenreich, 2010). In her search for advice on her situation, she found herself faced with an almost uniform approach advising her to fight the cancer through positive thinking. As a PhD in cellular biology, she found it hard to believe that her thinking could influence cells at a biological level, so she began to explore further the arguments behind these mind-over-matter assumptions. She concluded that evidence was weak and contradictory. Nonetheless, it affects people as she writes below:

> If you want to improve your life—both materially and subjectively— you need to upgrade you attitude, revise your emotional responses, and focus your mind. One could think of other possible means of self-improvement—through education, for example, to acquire new 'hard' skills, or by working for social changes that would benefit all. But in the world of positive thinking, the challenges are all interior and easily overcome through an effort of the will (Ehrenreich, 2010, p. 51).

Ehrenreich shows how unemployment, divorce, and even cancer are seen by positive thinkers as possibilities to develop and change. They are all viewed as things we can control. Ehrenreich claims that positive thinking has become a demand that affects everybody in Western societies as part of a historical development where individuals are seen as autonomous beings with responsibility for their thinking and thereby their conditions. Rereading the narrative gives me a sense that we all tried to control what was happening, and where affirmation was reduced to something, we could give to each other. The narrative contains several elements that displayed my inflated sense of control, where I thought I had control over the future, my feelings, and the feelings of others. I regarded affirmation as an entity I could give to Anna and the group to control their reactions. I felt Anna was doing the same to me. The idea that positive affirmation is something we can give to each other instrumentalises affirmation as something one can use to control the avoidance of feelings considered to be negative in oneself and others. This implies that we can predict how others will react and thereby control their reactions. I find that the narrative demonstrates the opposite. I believe that Anna had the best intentions of being nice to me and to protect me from being hurt. But it did not make me feel good at all. On the contrary, I felt ashamed and pitied.

The positive affirmation brought judgement of performance rather than a focus on shared experience from which we could learn. The influence of positive affirmation did not support that we engaged with emotions labelled as negative. I find it problematic that the continual affirmation of people and highlighting of success can lead to an unrealistic sense of individual responsibility, where we blame ourselves for failure and feel affirmed for events that we are not responsible for nor in control of. This resonates with the claims of positive thinking that, according to Ehrenreich, we have an inflated sense of control in regard to our own lives as well as in regard to other people.

At the start of this project, I thought that I, as an individual, was either in control or not in control. I struggled to be in control of the negotiations. And I was ashamed when I was not in control. Instead, I found the narrative shows that control was an ongoing negotiation about how to work together where the intentions of every participant interwove. Streatfield argues that, when organisations are understood from the perspective of complex responsive processes of relating, we cannot be 'in control' in a simple way. We must consider ourselves as being 'in control' and 'not in control' at the same time (Streatfield, 2001, p. 91).

Ehrenreich critiques the claims that control of our thinking in a positive direction will lead us to be successful and stand out as individuals. I will elaborate further on this need to stand out as individuals by drawing on the theory of the sociologist Norbert Elias.

Individuality

In Elias's view, we are all born into a world of relations that are already there when we arrive. We are thereby inseparable from others, and Elias uses the term *interdependent* to describe the weaving of our human ties (Elias, 1978, p. 77). This does not mean that we are not individuals each with our own identity. The more individuals are able to restrain and transform instinctive natural forces by love, fear of others, and self-control 'the more numerous and pronounced become the differences in their behaviour, their feelings, their thoughts, their goals, and not least their malleable physiognomies: the more "individualized" individuals become' (Elias, 2001, p. 140).

> In such societies it becomes a personal ideal of young people and adults to differ from others in one way or another, to distinguish oneself—in short, to be different. Whether he realizes it or not, in such societies, the individual is placed in a constant, partly tacit, partly explicit competitive struggle in which it is of utmost importance to his pride and self-respect. This ego-ideal of the individual, the desire to stand out from others, to stand on one's own feet and to seek fulfilment of a personal striving in one's own qualities, skills, possessions or achievements, is certainly a fundamental component of the individual person. It is something without which he would lose his identity in his own eyes as an individual (Elias, 2001, pp. 141–142).

When we enter the world at a specific time and place, certain patterns of relating have developed and Elias terms these patterns figurations (Elias, 1978, p. 130). He writes that neither we nor figurations are fixed entities; they are continually evolving. Elias writes further that exponents of individualism assume

that the life of a person, as they understand it—that is, the life of a
fundamentally isolated being hermetically sealed from the world—
must have a meaning, and perhaps even a preordained meaning,
solely in and for itself. Their quest for meaning is a quest for the
meaning of an individual person in isolation (Elias, 1986, p. 53).

Elias sees humans as thoroughly social and describes figurations where the
individual quest for meaning creates this need to stand out as an individual. In the
narrative, disappointment and shame affected my identity and perhaps that of the
group. I was emotionally affected by their rejection because it did not resonate
with the view I have of myself as someone who can achieve what he chooses to
pursue. The rejection was a threat to how I view myself, and it became much more
than the group's choice between different methods. In the instance in the
children's home in Project 1, a colleague at the doctoral programme suggested that
my strong reaction was due to a loss of control of how others evaluated my
performance. I appeared to position myself alone with the struggle, influenced by
an ideal of a stereotype of a lonely hero with the ability to solve the situation in
solitude. I agree with my colleague, and when I did not succeed, I reacted strongly
because my identity was challenged.

I find Elias's approach to figurations as shaping and being shaped through ongoing
relating compelling in explaining that we have an identity and lose aspects of that
same identity continuously. This understanding is more dynamic than traditional
psychological perspectives that view our personality as rather fixed through
processes of childhood experiences, biology, or behavioural conditioning (John,
Robins & Pervin, 1999). I instead understand Elias as seeing that identity is fixed
and not fixed at the same time. Elias describes how we often turn processes into
static conditions (Elias, 1978, p. 112). He shows how our use of language hides

processual aspects of a phenomenon leading us to handle processes as if they were an entity.

> We say, 'The wind is blowing,' as if the wind were actually a thing at rest which, at a given point in time, begins to move and blow. We speak as if the wind were separate from its blowing, as if a wind could exist which did not blow. This reduction of process to static conditions … we shall call 'process-reduction' for short (Elias, 1978, p. 112).

Stacey describes our understanding of thinking to show the idea of process-reduction as he compares thinking to walking. When we consider walking, we would never describe it as something that was inside our legs. It is the same regarding thinking that is embedded in ongoing social processes that involve other people (Stacey, 2003, p. 32). The narrative in this project shows that identity is being challenged, developed, and shaped in everyday interaction with others. The seemingly insignificant everyday meeting about a small job in the narrative caused me to feel a loss in terms of identity. I perceived their affirmation as a judgment about my identity; I struggled to hold on to my sense of self, and I was emotionally affected when events challenged my view of myself. This brings me to another of my animating questions concerning what happened when I felt a loss of control.

In short, I was advocating for less control, and they chose not to work in that way with me. I felt a lack of affirmation, and I experienced this as an emotional reaction. I experienced I was being pulled emotionally in different directions every time I turned a corner in the line of events: first, I was happy about the recommendation, then confused about what happened at the meeting, then surprised, disappointed, and ashamed when I was rejected, and finally, I was proud and happy when I was encouraged to apply for the position as manager. And it was not just one emotion at a time. As an example, I was happy to be encouraged to apply for the managerial position but at the same time anxious because it meant I would have to reject Anna. I believe that the participants in the group experienced shifting and mixed emotions too. I sensed they were curious about my approach, uncertain about what our working together might lead to, and uncomfortable about the unfamiliarity with my approach to how they normally worked. To understand emotions and how they are linked to control and affirmation, I will delve further into this.

Emotions and control

I have found the views expressed by Burkitt helpful in making sense of the relationship between emotions and control. He describes that emotions 'are multi-dimensional and cannot be reduced to biology, relations or discourses alone, but belong to all these dimensions as they are constituted in ongoing relational practices' (Burkitt, 1999, p. 115). With this view, he insists on a paradoxical view on emotions as shaping and being shaped by biology, relations, and discourse at the same time. In the following, I will write about these three dimensions and argue why I find this approach useful in understanding how control and emotions are linked and relational. I will supplement with other researchers who have written specifically about control and anxiety in organisational development.

Emotions as biology

Some of the emotions I experienced in the narrative are often called fundamental emotions. These emotions are termed happiness, surprise, sadness, anger, disgust, and fear. A psychology textbook describes how facial expressions reveal these fundamental emotions, and this theory relates to Darwin 'who considered these expressions to be vestiges of basic adaptive patterns shown by our evolutionary forerunners' (Gleitman, 1995, p. 443). The fundamental emotions are described as a universal basis in human emotions, and they are widely assumed in Western discourse. Wetherell traces a split between emotions and reason in Western discourse since the 19th century (2012, p. 104) where emotions are gradually viewed as more natural and reason as more controlled and rational. Burkitt (1999, 2012) argues that emotions are linked to the social and cannot be reduced to biology (1999, p. 115). Emotions might be individually felt but always arise in relations where they also express cultural norms and values (ibid, p. 122). 'Brain/body responses are autonomous only in the most limited senses and for all intents and purposes cannot be meaningfully separated from the rest of the assemblage that includes cultural, cognitive and conscious elements' (Wetherell, 2012, p. 62). Wetherell and Burkitt argues that emotions have a biological expression but contest the idea that there are fundamental emotions by arguing how emotions differ across cultures and, drawing on other neuroscientists, that the brain constantly develops in order to adapt and, therefore, does not consist of evolutionary fundamental emotions and newer parts that processes the older fundamental parts (ibid, p. 41). The views of Wetherell and Burkitt resonate with me in that the emotional experience in the narrative did not consist of one fundamental emotion at a time. It was experienced as a mix of different emotions that shifted frequently. Instead of focusing on single emotions, Gherardi argues for a focus on affect as the intensity: 'We want to think of affect as what colours an episode, an experience or a working practice, or as their intensity (Gherardi, 2017, p. 216). In my narrative, I was affected by a broad range of emotions as the events occurred, with the intensity signalling that something was important. With the perspective from Elias, I have found that my identity was at stake.

Emotions as discursive

Burkitt and Wetherell are very explicit in their views on emotions as bodily processes that cannot be reduced either to biology or to a purely discursive view as constructed primarily in language. 'One could say that a culture provides for people an *emotional habitus,* with a language and set of practices, which outline ways of speaking about emotions, and of acting out and upon bodily feelings within everyday life' (Burkitt, 1999, p. 117 Italics in original).

Burkitt draws on Elias in his view on emotions as discursive. Although the ideas of discourse and figuration are somewhat alike, I will use the term figuration in my continued exploration of control. This is because discourse is often understood, according to Burkitt, in a tradition of the French thinker Foucault who described how 'normative forms of regulation were located mainly in institutions that work to reform the body' (Burkitt, 1999, p. 4). I acknowledge that institutions, individuals and relations are intertwined but have chosen the term figuration to be clear in my terminology and in my reference to Elias' relational perspective on control and emotions in the local interactions in the narrative.

Disappointment and shame in a discursive perspective

So, how might emotions and control be understood in organisational development in the figurations I am a part of? When I was rejected, I was disappointed, and I have found research about disappointment helpful. Clancy et al. (2012) write about how disappointment is regarded as an unwanted feeling and how learning from situations that involve disappointment is limited. They argue that existing literature 'frames disappointment as a threat to organisational effectiveness … and as an emotion that needs to be managed in order to prevent it from damaging organisational morale and performance' (Clancy et al., 2012, p. 518). In their view, disappointment is experienced as a threat and a loss of stability that we try to avoid. They stress that the avoidance of disappointment, in line with Shaw's argument, hinders learning. In their research, they identify three different patterns of reactions to disappointment. Position 1 manages disappointment through self-withdrawal (I disappoint you), and position 2 manages disappointment through blame (I am disappointed with you). Clancy et al. argues that 'the first two positions create defensive ways of managing disappointment' (Clancy et al., 2012, p. 526). A view of disappointment as a loss that we can tolerate characterises position 3. 'Position 3 … reframes disappointment as tolerable rather than damaging' (Clancy et al., 2012, p. 526).

Clancy et al. write from a psychoanalytic tradition where they operate with a view on inner conflicts between biological drives and demands of control from an outer life. This is different from the views on interdependency I have advocated for earlier in this project. They also write about organisational learning as if organisations are entities that can learn themselves. As I have argued earlier, I find the paradoxical view on the individual and the social within the complex responsive processes perspective on relating more compelling than the separation of inner/outer and people/organisations. I choose to view the research of Clancy et al. on disappointment as a relevant explanation of patterns that emerge in the Western understanding of disappointment and not as a biologically inner driven conflict or as an idealised solution to turn negative feelings of disappointment into positive outcomes. This is why I explain it here as part of the understanding of emotions as discursive.

The pattern I recognise is that I was disappointed and directed the disappointment towards myself (position 1). In hindsight, I would have liked to tolerate the loss as described in position 3, but I felt not good enough, ashamed, and wanted to leave this negative experience behind. This links to shame that I find Curtis has written about. He argues that learning processes are necessarily linked to feelings of shame (Curtis, 2018, p. 48). It is in the nature of learning that we are exposed to our own ignorance and imperfection, and Curtis describes that, when we experience a loss of the power of knowing, we are challenged in our view of ourselves. When we are encountered with new knowledge, this results in individual feelings of shame. I will claim that both shame and disappointment are, as Fineman has described it, unwanted negative feelings that we tend to avoid in organisational work (2006), either by controlling outcomes or by suppressing the expression of negative feelings.

Emotions as relational

Shame and disappointment might be individually felt but, according to Burkitt, always arise in relations in specific figurations. He writes, 'We must not see these behaviours as "expressions" of any underlying thing called "emotion", for the expression *is* the emotion … *Expressions are not, then, the "outer" signal of "inner" feelings, but are signs in the networks of social relations and interdependencies'* (Burkitt, 1999, pp. 118–119, italics in original). With this perspective, the emotions that arose in the narrative were expressions of the relations within the group and with me. Burkitt suggests that relationships are the central object of study in research on emotions.

> I want to get away from the idea that emotions are expressions of something 'inner', so that the expression is an outer register of an inner process. Instead, I will claim that, if emotions are expressive of anything, it is of the relations and interdependencies that they are an integral part of, and in this sense emotions are essentially communicative: they are expressions occurring *between people* and registered on the body, rather than expressions of something contained inside a single person (Burkitt, 1999, p. 113, italics in original).

Burkitt's view of emotions as expressions *between people* makes me wonder how Anna and the rest of the group might have felt in the situation. Working with a looser structure was important to me but unfamiliar for both me and the group. Wetherell uses the phrase *affective practice* to describe our expectations and thereby what is familiar to us. 'An affective practice is a figuration where body possibilities and routines become recruited or entangled together with meaning-making and with other social and material figurations' (Wetherell, 2012, p. 17). In this way, emotions are not fundamental across contexts but are shaped and shape the affective practice. I view consultancy as an affective practice where we all had expectations as to how we were to work together and that this was negotiated. In our negotiations about how to work together in the narrative, I presented something unfamiliar, and this caused an emotional reaction. 'In other words, body states are always situated and always taking place in the midst of some activity, and the medium in which they are situated is culturally and socially constituted' (Wetherell, 2012, p. 42).

I have reflected upon this as I recognise that in the first five iterations of this project, I have been writing about what *I* did and how *I* felt, that *I* felt a loss of control, was disappointed and ashamed. When my colleagues at the DMan asked how the people in the group might have felt, I have found it difficult to provide plausible answers. In hindsight, I have reasoned that several of the participants' responses at the meeting suggest that they also sensed a loss of control about what the meeting and their supervision sessions would lead to, and they probably rejected me for that reason. However, I must admit that I had not paid much attention to how the group felt during the meeting. I have found myself embedded in an understanding of emotions as my own to an extent where I have found it difficult to take a relational view on what happened in the narrative. I found myself withdrawn as Clancy et al. suggest. In Burkitt's view, my emotions are expressions of relations and interdependencies, so if I am to make sense of emotions, I must understand our relations and how our relations developed. Therefore, I became increasingly interested in understanding what others felt and why they reacted as they did.

I tried to understand how Anna and her colleagues might have experienced the events with help from my colleagues on the DMan programme. Drawing on Larsen and Friis' work on improvising in research, I carried out a series of role plays with fellow researchers where we replayed the meeting (Larsen & Friis, 2017, p. 350). This allowed us to explore and reflect on how others might have experienced what happened. It triggered my curiosity further, and I decided to contact Anna again. One might say that I returned to her to have the conversation that I was too ashamed to have at the time of the events.

Meeting Anna again

I wrote and asked if she wanted to meet and explore what had happened at the meeting. She replied quickly that she found my inquiry interesting and we agreed to meet. We met at a café and our conversation started with a cheerful chat about the difficulties of remembering what had happened since the events passed by a year ago. Anna said she wanted to say that she was sad and disappointed that they had not chosen me as their supervisor but sadder that I had not applied for the job as their manager. I told her that her encouragement right after the rejection had made me uncertain about whether she encouraged me to try to cheer me up. She said that she had been honest. I asked what had made them decide on the other supervisor then. They had not discussed in depth why they chose the way they did. It was more like a vote. In Anna's experience, they had chosen the safe bet since the other candidate worked more familiarly. She was excited that supervision with me might be a way to discuss and explore things that they were not used to discussing. She found that her colleagues had not been courageous enough to try to work in a way that was not familiar to them. In her opinion, they were too afraid of the unknown, and this had disappointed her. I said I had been disappointed too. I was disappointed when I was rejected and too ashamed to explore why they had chosen the way they had. I felt some were anxious about my approach with less control but did not speak up about their concerns. She recognised that keeping quiet about negative views was a tendency in the group. She experienced that speaking up critically involved risks, with the risks being that you could be called to the manager's office for a correction, which a colleague had experienced very recently. There was also a risk of appearing incompetent and feeling marginalised with your views and excluded from the group. I said that I could also recognise a sense of being incompetent during my meeting with the group, as I suddenly recalled that, when I sensed scepticism from some of her colleagues, I mentioned I had written a book and was doing this doctoral degree. I mentioned this because I found it difficult to describe how I wanted to work, and I was afraid to come across as incompetent. In hindsight, I could have brought feelings of expectations and competency up with the group, but instead, I tried to act competent and confident. She also remembered this and told me that they had discussed it in the group afterwards. They had feared that they could not live up to my expectations. We both found it interesting that we all feared to come across as incompetent. As we finished our conversation, we shared that we had both found it interesting to engage in reflecting about what had happened.

Reflections on the conversation with Anna

Before the conversation, I feared it would have been an embarrassing conversation because of the rejection. I feared she would emphasise that I was incompetent, and this anticipation made me likely to avoid these conversations and the exploration of events that involve negative emotions. I see this avoidance as an attempt to control in order to preserve a certain view of myself. I had also sensed growing anxiety before we met because I had been working on this project for six months and, if Anna had presented entirely different views about what had happened, I felt I would have to rewrite my work. I experienced that this relational investigation was putting me in a position with less control of my project. However, I realised that I was, like in the meeting with the group, concerned about the outcome of the conversation rather than curious about what would happen. The reflections arising from this project made me think that it would be wrong if I rewrote parts of my work due to our café-conversation. Instead, I should reflect on our conversation no matter how different her perspectives would turn out to be. Regarding my meeting with Anna, one might say that I tried to change my narrative of being in control and instead explore her views on what happened. The loss of control in terms of facing potential embarrassment and towards the outcome of the meeting allowed me to explore the importance of emotions with Anna. The conversation with Anna supported the idea that emotions, like anxiety and disappointment, played a part for all of us. The conversation also directed my attention to the fear of coming across as incompetent as something we all shared. I find that this fear is linked to a preservation of identity that I described with reference to the work of Elias.

So, how did the conversation with Anna contribute to my exploration of control? In the conversation with Anna, I experienced that it was valuable to the understanding of what happened to share how we felt. The conversation also led me to correct my doubts about Anna's sincerity and my suspicion that she was soothing me. The conversation made me reflect that, initially, I thought the narrative was about my failure either to convince them or to compromise between their and my ways of working. But I found that when I left the idea that it was about success or failure, the narrative offered me a way to explore what happened. In terms of my identity, getting the job probably would have brought me positive affirmation that supported my view of myself. And if it had not been for the exploration in this project, I would have avoided engaging further with Anna or the group in order to forget it as a shameful experience. This way, neither getting the job nor being rejected would have resulted in reflections on my identity and learning from my experience. My tendency to seek positive affirmation would have made me struggle to reproduce my view of myself and my way of working. The view on emotions as relational and the conversation with Anna allowed me to conclude that returning to what seemed to be a failure involved important learning. This brings me to conclude that control involves relational emotions. The relational view allows us to explore what is important to all of us. We all had feelings of disappointment and incompetence. We registered them differently on our bodies because we are different individuals with different position and intentions: For Anna, the different view on control was important because it allowed for new discussions in the group. For several members of the group, it involved unfamiliarity and anxiety. I find myself beginning to explore emotions in my practice as a consultant where I share my feelings and encourage others to do the same. In this way, I am changing my practice, and I realise that my identity changes with this.

Control, emotions, and relations

How has the relational view on emotions developed my understanding of why control is important? I find that my reflections, literature, role plays, and the conversation with Anna supported a relational view as we all experienced emotions and anxiety as well as excitement, that was linked to control.

Regarding emotions and control, Fineman and Sturdy refer to *emotions of control* in their article of the same title (1999). They argue that control is considered an emotional response in a specific social context. They claim that 'the emotional texture of control is an essential condition and outcome of apparent agreements and personal commitments' (Fineman & Sturdy, 1999, p. 651). My exploration supports this relational perspective on control and emotions where control is relational and concerns the interweaving of intentions rather than one person controlling others. The need to control arises because individuals preserve a sense of a certain identity. The relational perspective involves a loss of control since it is not possible to have control over a social process. I realise that I have regarded control to be an individual ability, and trying to control an emotion might be, as Wetherell writes, as difficult as trying to control a sneeze (Wetherell, 2012, p. 42). Instead, I will argue, as Streatfield does, that control is not something one person can have.

> The complex responsive process perspective … is one that avoids collapsing thought to either the "in control" or the "not in control" pole (Streatfield, 2001, p. 129).

This does not mean that we are entirely out of control either, and in line with Streatfield, I will argue that we must see ourselves as being 'in control' and 'not in control' at the same time. In the narrative, I tried to control and suppress the emotions, and in this project, I have tried to explore what the emotions were expressions of, from a relational perspective of control. We all tried to maintain control by giving and receiving positive affirmation. The glorification of positive thinking depreciates negatively labelled feelings of shame and disappointment and thereby limits our desire to inquire into events that involve these feelings. The relational perspective on emotions has led me to believe that incompetence, shame, disappointment, anxiety, or the fear of these feelings are inseparable from control as expressions of relations.

The argument so far

Here is a summary of the argument so far on why control is important in organisational development. I chose to explore a narrative where I was, to my surprise, emotionally affected. I was advocating for an approach in which I would control less. I wanted to work in new ways but, at the same time, struggled to keep my view of myself as someone who can control that I get what I want and be positively affirmed. Positive affirmation was the currency in my evaluation of events, and this limited how I engaged with the negative emotions in the experience. In the perspective expressed by Shaw, I might have failed to pay attention to the level of anxiety that the looser structure provided. In that sense, I did not find a compromise where I adapted to others so that we could have moved on and worked together. I might not have given up my interests in a looser structure, but rather have started more flexibly. The inquiries in this project have made me aware of the lengths we all went to in our efforts to affirm and be affirmed. One might say that our need for positive affirmation and to affirm others in order to control a desired future controlled us instead. I became aware of this pattern in Project 1, and although I tried to work in ways where I lost control, I repeated patterns where I was dependent on positive affirmation to stand out as an individual. When positive affirmation is used as a tool, it entails that one situates oneself in a position to judge others.

I inquired into research on emotions and found resonance with Burkitt who views emotions as biology, social relations, and discourse paradoxically formed and being formed as complexes. I have explored disappointment and shame as specific unwanted emotions, and I have found they are important parts of learning processes but are, for reasons explained in contemporary Western figurations involving positive thinking, often suppressed in my experience. Thereby we are reluctant to explore negatively labelled emotions in social interactions since this might challenge our view of ourselves as individuals who stand out from each other. I have argued that affect, which I see as the intensity of emotions, signifies that something is important to our identity and how we might react to this as a threat to our view on ourselves. The narrative shows that, in local interactions such as negotiations about how to work together, this dynamic involves identity and how identity thereby continuously changes and stays the same. This invokes a view on identity as paradoxically stable and unstable at the same time. I plan to explore and clarify this further later in this thesis.

Further research

I have begun to pay more attention to how positive affirmation affects what I and others do and why we do it. I have come to see that my purpose as a consultant is not to make everybody feel good if this is at the cost of focusing on the content of work and reflecting on what happens. I find myself embedded in a practice of relating in organisational development where positive affirmation is used to control the avoidance of anxiety and to achieve specific outcomes. When it is used deliberately, I have found that positive affirmation might be disparaging and judgmental as it might cut our self and others off from reflecting on important issues.

Leaving the comfort of tools and techniques in organisational development felt like a loss of control that aroused feelings of anxiety both in the group and me. Stacey argues that one of the purposes of tools and techniques in organisational work is to create predictable patterns to reduce anxiety (Stacey, 2012). Tools like the reflecting team method might be necessary to create enough familiarity and comfort to explore conflicts, and it might also be a requirement for some jobs. So, I might have to compromise and use my experience to assess what to do in each situation. This means I will pay more attention to people's anxiety. Not in order to avoid feelings of anxiety but to allow us to move on and then reflect on it together.

I see that my job as a consultant is to reflect with my clients about what we do and why we do it as a participant where I take responsibility for what I do from my specific position which must be negotiated with the participants. This has left me curious to understand how to be responsible without being an organisational development expert who can control outcomes through concepts, strategic plans, personality profiles, and models. I see my purpose as a consultant to allow for all to take experience seriously together.

With this view, the notion of responsibility changes and I wish to explore ways to understand and act responsibly in interactions with others. In Project 3, I want to delve further into ways to work together where we lose control but still act responsibly and take others seriously.

Project 3: Consultancy and impression management

In Project 2, I paid attention to emotions and affirmation regarding control. I concluded that control is not a commodity one can possess, and I will explore control, emotions, and affirmation further in my work with a group of managers where I was hired to reflect with them on their management practice. However, before I turn to the narrative, I will describe an experience from my personal life because it reveals how my thinking about control in consultancy is changing.

Control in my personal life

In April 2018, while I was writing Project 2, my mother was diagnosed with pancreatic cancer in a progressed stage. Immediately after the diagnosis, she started treatment but was informed that this was only for palliative purposes and that she should not expect to live long. I cancelled as much as I could workwise and planned to visit her often. I had expected that the period with cancer would be a calm and intimate period with conversations about our lives and shared experiences. But the cancer's pace seemed unreal and within weeks of the diagnosis she was tired, nauseated, and had little energy for conversations. Two months earlier she had appeared healthy, and I was left in a state of shock. Immediately after the diagnosis, I was shifting between intense grief and forgetting she was ill. When I was reminded of her illness, I felt guilty that I was not sadder. It was as if my feelings were not mine but were invading my body from time to time. I found this very uncomfortable. I could not act to change what would inevitably happen and felt confused because I could not control my feelings. She died two months after the diagnosis. At the very end, it was a relief that she found peace but, unfortunately, much too soon.

I found that my feelings invaded my work too. For example, I had a series of conversations with a manager who was affected by the recent loss of her son. In that situation, I could not hold my tears back, and I explained that I was sorry for her loss and that her grief resonated with me because my mother was terminally ill at the time. I felt that I was being unprofessional. The fear that Streatfield expressed in the following resonates with me: 'When we go to work we try to remove emotions from the workplace, believing that if they are expressed they will open up a Pandora's box of not being in control' (2001, p. 8). When I cried in the conversation with the manager, I did not experience that a Pandora's box was opened though. I found that we had an intimate and moving session where she felt I had taken her seriously, and it helped us both to explore how we might understand feelings of grief. This took place as I was making sense of the events in the narrative in Project 2 and contributed to my curiosity towards the exploration of feelings. I often find a pattern where both my clients and I expect me to analyse, understand, and master difficult situations that will lead us to a desired future. I have tried to live up to this image both as a consultant and manager, and I thought that theories and methods would enable me to control and navigate successfully in the situations I would encounter.

In the light of my reflections around my mother's death and my experience in writing Project 2, I have noticed how my practice is gradually changing. I have chosen to describe the following narrative, which took place at the same time as my mother's illness because it shows how my increased attention towards feelings in organisational work affected what we did together. However, the events also puzzled me because they did not solve our problems and drew my attention to underlying assumptions behind what I was doing in my practice as a consultant.

Narrative: Disappointment in the management group

The narrative revolves around four meetings with the top management in a private organisation for health care for older adults spread out over Denmark. I had been hired by Carl, the director, in June 2017 after I had met with him and the four managers who reported directly to Carl. They wanted to reflect on what they were doing and why they were doing it in order to fulfil their task of taking care of the older citizens. They wanted to explore how they worked together as a group and how they could continually learn from their experience. My assignment involved monthly meetings with the group where I should reflect on the above with them.

In our meetings, we found a pattern of working in which I usually started with a short presentation on a topic that we had agreed on in the previous meeting, such as management dilemmas or their intentions for the organisation. After the presentation, we would reflect on their everyday practice, and I was thereby shifting between teaching and participating in reflections with them. I experienced that we were reflecting on what we were doing and why we were doing it as I aspired to in Project 2. I felt less of a performer and more like a participating explorer into how they worked together. Carl and his managers were happy about our work together and even expressed that they had been able to talk about their leadership for the first time as a group. I was soothed by their affirmation and thought to myself that this was a great way to work. I felt relieved that I need not set out a tight timetable, pull out a model or a clever response but also slightly guilty for not doing so. Could this be a way of working that customers would find valuable? Their continual hiring of me for monthly meetings suggested that it was. However, our work gradually changed as I will describe in the following.

Meeting 1: The Local Cohesion meeting

Towards the end of our monthly meeting in March 2018, Carl explained that he felt pressure from the board to present a clear and visible direction for the organisation. In his opinion, 'local cohesion' would be the answer to their needs.

This would imply a closer collaboration between the four manager's areas so that the rehabilitation and development units would be more present in the nursing homes and share their resources to a much higher degree. We had time for only a short discussion about what he meant, and I suggested that I could prepare a presentation about local cohesion for the following meeting. Carl asked if I could also produce a note about local cohesion and a rough plan about how to implement it in the rest of the organisation. I agreed. As I was preparing the note, I noticed that a different feeling of responsibility was sneaking up on me. I felt responsible for guiding the organisation in a certain direction instead of reflecting together with Carl and the managers as we were accustomed to. I did not think further about it though and did my best to produce a plan.

Meeting 2: The disappointment meeting

I sent the note and briefly presented it at the meeting. Shortly after we had engaged in a discussion, Carl stood up and spoke without interruption for around five minutes. He was frustrated that the managers were not already working on local cohesion in the organisation. He had pointed out how important it was back in March and, in his opinion, nothing had happened since. A knot tightened in my stomach. I did not like the tension, and I felt shame for not living up to his expectations. When I looked at the managers, they looked shameful too. They were quiet and looked down at the tables in front of them.

When he paused, there was silence before I intervened and said I was sorry if I had misunderstood him, but I had found it difficult to plan in further detail before we had discussed what local cohesion meant. The managers nodded in approval and looked at Carl.

He sat down in a chair and sighed. He said that the lack of progress must be his fault since, apparently, he had not explained his intentions clearly enough. He apologised for his emotional outburst but emphasised that we needed to act on local cohesion in the organisation because he sensed that the board was getting impatient to see some action. No one spoke for a while, and I intervened again to suggest that we could start to work on a timetable. We did so, and the meeting ended shortly after.

After the meeting, I was puzzled. Previously, I had found the managers keen to do what Carl wanted, but they came across as unusually passive, and Carl was unexpectedly temperamental. Why did these feelings of disappointment and shame arise? In hindsight, I think I interrupted the silence and suggested that we embark on planning activities to mitigate Carl's frustration. Also, I think the managers were perplexed about what he wanted and supported my suggestion as a way out of the emotionally tense situation.

At that time, I was writing about so-called negative emotions in Project 2, and I found that disappointment was an emotion that affected me quite strongly, not in an open aggressive way but as an internal turmoil that sparked reactions about being good enough and shameful. Due to my reflections in Project 2, I decided to explore what the disappointment during the meeting might express about what was going on between us. I felt Carl should approve bringing it up, so I called and asked him about it. He said it would be very interesting to explore our emotional patterns but added that it was important that it could only last for 30 minutes since he wanted to use the rest of the meeting, two hours, to plan the implementation of local cohesion in the organisation. I would have liked more time for the exploration of emotions, but I did not share this with Carl. However, I thought the sharp separation between reflections and planning might symptomatically express how negative emotions are something to be fixed as an isolated item on an agenda. I accepted the timeframe as a compromise since we also had subsequent meetings where we could continue our exploration of patterns of shame and disappointment. I was also afraid that he would be irritated or disappointed with me if I kept challenging his need to plan the implementation. Besides, I could not think of an alternative to producing a plan.

Meeting 3: The reflection meeting

As the meeting started, I described how disappointment, according to Clancy et al. (2012), can turn into a blame game and moved on to describe my experience in the last meeting where Carl was disappointed, the rest of us quiet, and Carl taking the blame in the end. I had felt shameful during the meeting, and I wondered whether others had a similar experience.

The managers spoke one at a time. Two of them said they had felt shameful, and they all recognised an emotionally awkward stuckness that they wanted to move away from. After their round, we all looked at Carl. There was a short pause, but when he said he found this discussion important and valuable, I sensed the rest of us felt relieved. He said he would pay close attention to how disappointment might express something important for us to explore. We discussed it for 30 minutes as planned, and it was as if the air had been cleared. The rest of the meeting progressed with an easy flow of contributions and discussions. We planned that the four managers should initiate conversations with their lower-level managers about what they needed to do to work with local cohesion. We also agreed that I should further develop the implementation plan with activities and goals.

When I left the meeting, I called and left a message with Carl to hear how he had experienced the meeting. Earlier in my career, I would have worked to create a positive atmosphere and avoid conflicts; I would not have shared my thoughts the way I did with the risk of arousing conflicts in which people might get hurt or angry with me. I would have argued that conflicts were not productive, and I would probably have drawn on appreciative inquiry, as described in Project 2, to avoid conflicts in my attempts to create a better future for the participants. Instead, I had explored our emotions, which was unfamiliar to me. So, when Carl wrote that I had done a great job, I was very pleased. In hindsight, I think I called Carl because I was also curious to hear if he was happy about my performance.

Meeting 4: The second disappointment meeting

I sent my draft for implementing local cohesion a week before our meeting. Due to the geographical distance in the organisation, Carl was participating via the phone, which caused distractions since he was disturbed and hung up several times. He also, probably unwillingly, interrupted the row of speakers since he could not see who was preparing to speak. After I had presented the plan, the managers said they had launched discussions of the topic in their areas as agreed. Carl interrupted and said that he was getting frustrated again. He needed more action now. He was disappointed that the managers had not yet created more cooperation between the nursing homes and rehabilitation. He reminded us how he had been stressing the importance since March and that the board might order massive restructuring of the organisation if sufficient action was not shown. Carl said he was aware that he was repeating the pattern of disappointment we had discussed, but he could not help it. I also felt he was disappointed with my plan, and I felt ashamed about it. I recognise a pattern where I feel responsible for the positive development of events and, therefore, take the blame when things evolve differently from that. But this time was slightly different because I was also irritated and disappointed that we found ourselves stuck in a pattern of disappointment again. These feelings were different from the first disappointment meeting but also a change in my response that I ascribe to the greater awareness of emotions in my practice.

The time had run out, and Carl finished his call. One of the managers had to leave and looked confused and intimidated as she left. The remaining managers and I were quiet and baffled before we discussed why the pattern had recurred. I said I understood Carl's frustration if he experienced that nothing had happened on the one hand. On the other hand, I thought, like the managers, that further steps needed to be developed together and that actions were already in motion in the organisation. The latter perspective was not clearly conveyed by any of us in the meeting, and I think this was due to Carl's emotionally intense expression.

As I left, I was puzzled about what I was doing as a consultant. Was I a participant reflecting on what was going on, a consultant to guide processes that would help their reflections, or was I an expert consultant planning the future for them? My role had gradually changed towards the latter, and since this was not how we had agreed to work initially or what I wanted, I wondered why. I even wondered what consultants are supposed to do.

Initial reflections on the narrative

Earlier, I have seen myself as a neutral expert who could turn things to the positive through my facilitation of processes. I have found myself gradually being closer to my clients, sharing my feelings and revealing more of myself both in and between meetings. As I argued in Project 2, feelings are not only biological individual inner states but are relational expressions. When Carl experienced pressure from the board and wanted more local cohesion, the emotions grew intense. I responded to this by trying to help his need to plan the implementation of more local cohesion. I shifted from reflecting *with* them to working *for* Carl to create more local cohesion. It seemed terribly important for me to help Carl in his efforts and to not let him down. Why was it so important for me not to disappoint Carl that I diverged from how I wanted to work?

My colleagues on this DMan programme suggested that I was not only adapting to Carl's wishes but also to my expectations about what I should accomplish as a consultant. Since I was disappointed when the disappointment pattern recurred, I had expected the pattern to dissolve. My colleagues made me realise that I still expected to control the process in a way that would lead us to harmonious cooperation and a positive state of mind. In a sense, I was trying to control events with the use of feelings, and I still find myself influenced by assumptions behind consultancy I have previously practised. Therefore, I will start to explore broader patterns of consultancy within organisational development to understand why I reacted the way I did.

Process Consulting

In the past, before I embarked on the DMan programme, I identified myself as a 'process consultant'. Schein coined this as an ideal form of consultancy to develop organisations. He argued that successful consultancy requires that the consultant is not an expert pointing at specific solutions for the organisations they worked in but should instead support the client's ability to intervene in their own practice (1987, p. 29; 2006, p. 294). The reason for this is that the members of an organisation can come up with the best solutions and also that they will resist change if an outsider tries to create it. This brings in another of Schein's famous ideas, that of organisational culture. Schein argued that any organisation is a system with a culture that holds assumptions and that any change in organisations would interfere with these (Schein, 2017, p. 22). So, assumptions are not variables one can merely alternate at will, and the creation of successful changes have to come from the client system itself. Consultancy was no longer about designing organisations; instead it is about designing processes of reflection with a broad range of conversational tools and methods. He argues that process consulting is driven by the client's agenda and is about turning the members of the organisation into experts on their problems (Schein, 1995, p. 14). In this process, the consultant must adapt an anthropological perspective and see the client's culture from a 'native point of view' to change dysfunctional elements (Schein, 2006, p. 299). To make this happen, the client needs to trust the consultant because 'the client will typically not tell the helper what is really the problem until he or she trusts the helper to be helpful' (Schein, 1995, p. 18). Schein emphasises that the goal of process consulting is to establish a helping relationship with the client (1999, p. 1). If consultants do not hold on to this position, it 'not only lets the client off the hook as a learner but allows the client to 'blame' the consultant if things do not work out' (Schein, 1995, p. 16) while also making the consultant less responsible for what happens.

Process consultancy is located in the broader tradition of organisational development (OD) (e.g., French & Bell, 1995), and Schein, like many other OD scholars, draws on appreciative inquiry (AI) (Schein, 1999, p. 56). In Project 2, I described how AI relies on a social constructionist view and claims that we can create a positive future through language (Cooperrider & Srivastva, 1987, p. 36). Cooperrider and Srivastva claim that 'the future is ours—together—to shape and create' (2013, p. 15). Process consultancy and AI have been developed further in contemporary OD. Bushe is an influential author in this strand and has termed his approach 'dialogic organisation development' (2015). Dialogic OD works to instil a positive mindset into organisations and people (Maxton & Bushe, 2018, p. 425). 'Dialogic approaches work by fostering generativity to develop new possibilities rather than problem-solving, altering the prevailing narratives and stories that limit new thinking, and working with the self-organizing, emergent properties of complex systems' (Bushe & Marshak, 2016, p. 407). Dialogic OD offers a broad variety of structured conversational activities aimed at changing what words, stories, and narratives mean in the organisation (ibid, p. 409). Process consultation, AI, and dialogic OD persistently describe organisations as systems and share assumptions with second-order systemic ideas about the consultant as a person standing outside what is happening, as described in the following by Campbell. 'Systemic thinking is a means by which people can step back and observe their own position in the system' (Campbell, 1995, p. 20).

In sum, process consulting, AI and dialogic-OD shares a view on organisations as systems. They share the assumptions that you can deliberately change the way people talk and think to the positive through pre-planned tools or conversational guides. They differ with regard to the extent to which they see the consultant as standing outside the system they are trying to change or whether they are participants. Still, they all hold the assumption that the consultant must take the position of a helper who can bring in the right tool for the specific situation. These tools serve as a vehicle to control the direction of the conversation, and thereby how people think, in a positive direction. I will return with a critique of the practice and the intellectual assumptions behind these theories later in this project. I have presented it here to understand my practice and how the managers in the narrative and I were influenced by this practice. I will describe how this played out in the narrative.

Earlier in my practice as a consultant and manager, I have drawn on this body of knowledge, believing that skilled process consultants could control processes to create a positive mindset in others. I have worked to position myself in a helping position, and I can relate to this as my strong need to avoid blame in my work. In Project 1, I described how I was happy that I was not the responsible consultant on the stage when criticism arose in the appreciative inquiry process. However, as my practice is gradually changing, and I have been sharing my feelings as I did in the introduction about my mother's death, I feel more responsible for what happens. I have begun to question how process consulting advocates avoidance of blame and responsibility.

In the narrative, I think I engaged in planning activities to avoid being blamed by Carl, and I will describe how I was influenced by process consulting because, although I wanted to work in a more participatory way, I ended working in accordance with the ideas of process consulting when I felt blamed due to Carl's disappointment.

Process consulting in the narrative

I began by working in a less controlling and more participative approach in the narrative where I participated in the dialogue with my experience and feelings without having in mind particular results for our discussions. However, when I expected to create a more harmonious atmosphere, I was clearly influenced by process consultation, AI, and dialogic OD, and I experienced the same problems in the process of creating local cohesion in the narrative that I had already experienced as a manager in Project 1 and as a consultant in Project 2. I did not succeed in designing processes of reflection that created positive mindsets or helped to create a desired future. Instead, we were all caught up in being disappointed with each other and ourselves. While Carl was trying to control results, influenced by ideas about engineering the future, I was struggling to change our dialogues to the positive. All this makes me wonder; are consultants not supposed to help clients?

Taking my experience seriously in the DMan research community has spurred my questioning of the assumptions behind process consulting. I have argued that we need to pay attention to how we try to control the future because this influences our reflections. I am not saying that we do not have intentions and that managers should not try to influence events in a certain direction, but the narrative shows how attempts to control the future made us stuck and caught up in patterns of disappointment instead of reflecting together about our intentions and what was going on.

Human interaction and unpredictability

I find the American pragmatist George Herbert Mead helpful in explaining how it is impossible to control the future because, although we anticipate what might happen, we cannot control or predict how others behave and how their behaviour will affect us (1934, p. 7). Mead, with his idea of *the generalised other* (ibid, p. 154), proposed an original approach to explain how we continually develop as we are responsive to others. He argued that we are radically intertwined with other people from birth and that we learn to understand ourselves through the reactions our gestures bring out in others. As we gradually extend the number of people we relate to, we take the attitude of groups of more and more others which we generalise. The anticipated response we might get then influences our gestures, and this allows us to anticipate the response of others with some predictability. But we can never be certain about how others will respond and how we will then respond to their response. Mead explains how the ongoing relating between people, where our interpretation of the past and anticipations towards the future simultaneously affect our understanding of the present. Shaw describes this as 'the living present' (2002, p. 46). In this understanding of time, all three tenses coexist. Expectations and interpretations of the past influence what happens in the present

(Mead, 1932, p. 11), and our anticipations towards the future affect the present and thereby how we understand the past, which will change in the future, as cited by Mowles (2011, p. 200). Experience must be viewed in relation to time. This means that we can never recall events as they were because we will always think about them through the lens of where we are now. Thereby Mead challenges the separation between past, present, and future and the assumption that the past determines the present that then determines the future. This corresponds to Elias's idea of social life comprising the interweaving of intentions as a way to understand how no one can control the intention of other people since everybody has intentions and our dependency on each other is part of how we interact and how events play out (Elias, 1978, p. 77). Therefore, we cannot control our own intentions either. They will be influenced by interaction with others. I thereby argue that because of the unpredictability of peoples gestures and responses, the future is uncertain, so the idea that anyone can be in control of the future or other people's intentions is flawed.

I take this to mean that our meetings in the narrative were part of a wider and ongoing process which includes our prior individual experiences and our history together, other people's agendas, and broader expectations towards our practice. Instead of trying to control the future to the positive, I could have insisted on reflecting on what local cohesion might mean for their organisation, for themselves as a group, and how this might influence their way of working together. None of us paid attention to how we were conditioned by each of our specific past experiences in regard to local cohesion. We did not explore why the pattern of disappointment recurred and thereby how it was formed in the living present. My learning set also drew attention to my history with the group and how my assignment was long-term. I recognise how I was gradually identifying myself as an employee, similar to the position of the managers responding to this by trying to do what Carl wanted instead of reflexively engaging in our work together.

In sum, I claim that organisational change is a continual process where our relations, our interpretation of the past, and our anticipation of the future affect what we do in the living present. This continual process also involves our response to ideas about what consultants and managers are supposed to do, and I find Mead's idea about social objects helpful in exploring this further (1925).

Process Consulting as a social object

Mead argues that we respond to social objects in ways similar to how we respond to physical objects, although we have to be more responsive to a social object (which we co-create) than we do to a natural object. A social object is the generalised tendency, common to many people, to act habitually in similar ways (1925, pp. 265–266). In the narrative, I will argue that we all responded to process consulting as a social object, people have for each other in the narrative. I found myself between an ideology that implies a detached, helping, conflict-free, and cooperative position as a consultant holding individual skills (Bushe & Marshak, 2015; Schein, 1988) and one that involves the consultant as a reflexively engaged participant drawing attention to power relations we are all part of, which involves conflicting interests. The view on power is an important difference between process consulting and the perspective of complex responsive processes of relating, and there is more to explore in terms of power and my practice as a consultant. I plan to return to this in the next project. But first, I will sum up on the differences I have outlined so far.which means a set of shared expectations that influenced us. They had particular expectations of me as the kind of consultant they might have become used to, a process consultant. I will explore in the narrative what characterises the social object of process consulting that influenced us.

In my description of process consulting as a social object, I relate to my own experience and the theories I brought in earlier in this project to describe the practice of process consulting as individually learned skills that can be applied in different contexts. Organisations are viewed as systems in which consultants can teach the members to solve their problems. It is presented as a generalisable, decontextualised and ahistorical approach that applies to all organisations. This implies that the consultant can view the system from the outside and decide what to do. It is ritualised through the consultant's orchestration of structured activities, plans, models, grids, icebreakers, and games. In my exploration of the events in the narrative, I have grown increasingly curious about the assumptions behind process consulting, and as I have mentioned, I have found a critical perspective that offers alternative explanations to what consultants might be doing in organisations. Therefore, I will turn to Ralph Stacey and a group of his colleagues who draw on the ideas of Mead and Elias, among others, to continually develop what is termed 'the perspective of complex responsive processes of relating'.

The perspective of complex responsive processes of relating

Before I joined the DMan, I read the works of Ralph Stacey, and I was intrigued by his argument that, since interactions with others are predictably unpredictable, it is impossible to control social processes in general and organisational development in particular (Stacey, 2001). This approach is based on insights from complexity sciences, process sociology (e.g., as described by Elias), American pragmatism (primarily influenced by Dewey and Mead), and group analysis (as described by Foulkes) and has been developed as a body of knowledge and practice (Stacey & Mowles, 2016). Stacey and Mowles take seriously the idea that human relating is not a temporal linear exchange of gestures and responses and, in line with Mead, the idea that experience cannot be seen as a causal series of events located in the brain (1934, p. 32). They adopt Mead's fundamentally opposite position regarding the mechanical stimulus-response model proposed by classical behaviourists in his time (ibid, p. 8).

> The social act … is not explained by building it up out of stimulus plus response; it must be taken as a dynamic whole—as something going on—no part of which can be considered or understood by itself—a complex organic process implied by each individual stimulus and response involved in it (Mead, 1934, p. 7).

This dynamic whole entails that individuals are part of complex organic processes and are intertwined into relationships with others that cannot be untwined. Individuals are radically social, and we can never separate ourselves and our thinking from others completely (Stacey, 2003). At the same time, Mead stresses that we as humans can take ourselves as an object so that, when we are gesturing to others, we are also gesturing to ourselves. Self-consciousness is the ongoing process of taking ourselves as an object. 'We appear as selves in our conduct in so far as we ourselves take the attitude that others take toward us … We take the rôle of what may be called the "generalized other." And in doing this, we appear as social objects, as selves' (Mead, 1925, pp. 268–269). This also means that humans are reflexive beings. Mowles describes that reflexivity 'calls into question how we know what we know and how we have come to know it … We "bend back" (*reflectere*) our thinking on itself and on ourselves in order to call into question our own role in understanding what it is we are trying to understand' (Mowles, 2015, pp. 60–61 Italics in original). We are not just subjected to and constrained by others or the figurations we are born into. We have the ability to be reflexive about how we are constrained.

The perspective of complex responsive processes of relating, originally developed by Stacey and Griffin, stresses the importance of power as we relate to others and draws on Elias's description of power:

> Whether the power differentials are large or small, balances of power are always present wherever there is functional interdependence between people. In this respect, simply to use the word 'power' is likely to mislead. We say that a person possesses great power as if power were a thing he carried about in his pocket… Power is not an amulet possessed by one person and not by another;

> it is a structural characteristic of human relationships—of all human
> relationships (Elias, 1978, p. 74).

So, a person does not have power as if it was a thing. Power is an enabling-
constraining relationship that depends on the relative need people have for each
other (Stacey & Griffin, 2005, p. 9). It is a characteristic in the perspective of
complex responsive processes of relating that we are paradoxically constrained and
enabled at the same time, that we adjust to an environment and become a
different individual because of this adjustment. But in becoming a different
individual, we also change the environment. This explains how we are formed by
and, at the same time, forming local as well as global patterns (Mead, 1934, p.
215). 'One can only really understand an organisation from within the local
interaction in which global tendencies to act are taken up' (Stacey & Griffin, 2005,
p. 9). This means that I can explore global patterns in consultancy through the
exploration of the interactions in the narrative. In the narrative, I tried to work as a
participant with less preplanning and no pre-made conversational guides or models
to explore what we were doing and why we were doing it, inspired by the
perspective of complex responsive processes of relating. But at the same time, I
was also responding to the social object of process consulting. In the following, I
will explore their differences.

Differences between Process Consulting and Complex Responsive Processes

It is assumed that consultants who are responding to the social object of process
consulting can stand outside, observe, and pick the right tool for the intervention
to control others to the positive. Mowles argues that 'the dominant theory of
consultancy or managerial intervention in organisations is based on systems
dynamics where there is an assumption both that an organisation is a self-
regulating system and that the consultant/manager is a detached, objective
observer who can intervene to help staff bring about specific and necessary

change' (Mowles, 2011, p. 31). I was inspired by the perspective of complex responsive processes of relating where consultants are not viewed as separate from others in the organisation without the ability to observe others from the outside as if they are not a part of what is going on (Stacey, 2003, p. 120). This is displayed in the narrative where I could not observe what was going on from an outside position, let alone control it to the positive.

The inability to control processes resonates with my experience, and although this is a relief because I do not have to feel responsible for the outcome of events which I am not in control of, it is also anxiety-provoking because consultancy often implies a promise about certain results or the creation of positive mindsets. And the more grandiose the claims about how positive the future will be, the bigger the potential for disappointment. Fineman argues that organisational theorising has taken a positive turn (2006, p. 270), and I argue that this means we breed disappointment that moreover, in the light of this positive turn, is difficult to explore. Our response to disappointment expresses global patterns of expectations about how emotions are expressed in the practice of consultancy (Burkitt, 1999). As I described in Project 2, Wetherell coined the term 'affective practice' to describe how practices involve certain emotional patterns (2012, p. 4). I argue that the affective practice related to the social object of process consulting is one that prescribes a helping, conflict-free, and cooperative relationship with clients. This was present in the narrative when I tried to create a positive atmosphere, and although I brought attention to feelings of disappointment, I withdrew and did not explore the disappointment in both of the meetings where Carl expressed disappointment with strong emotions. The perspective of complex responsive processes of relating draws attention to what we are doing in the living present, which involves our history of local cohesion and why it turned out to be difficult. Although we had agreed to work together in a way where we would reflect on what we were doing and why we were doing it, we slipped into the habits of planning, implementing, and instilling positive attitudes in others when Carl was under pressure from the board. One way to think of this is in terms of what Mead calls social control. 'In so far as there are social acts, there are social objects, and I take it that social control is bringing the act of the individual into relation with this social object' (Mead, 1925, p. 273). I understand Mead in the way that I brought myself to relate as an employee and to the social object of process consulting in the narrative as a social control to create stability when Carl was anxious about whether he was delivering results to the board. And again, I wonder how this response might also be in relation to Carl's position of power.

I have argued that it was not helpful when I slipped into the role of process consulting trying to create positive mindsets because it distracted us from exploring our specific history of local cohesion and what that might mean for us, including how we related both to the social object of process consulting and how my long-term relation made me feel responsible for delivering a certain outcome. This might have made me call Carl before the meeting, allowing him to choose whether I should present my experience of their patterns of disappointment or not. I called because he was the client but also because I was seeking his affirmation and these gestures amplified that I acted in a way that ascribed control to Carl and supported the power relation with him in charge. This distracted us from critically exploring the intentions behind local cohesion. When I took the task of planning local cohesion, I might have, unwillingly, made the managers wait for my plan before taking further actions which might have reinforced Carl's disappointment.

Controlling the future through visions and plans

We acted as if the idea of local cohesion came from Carl due to pressure from the board and that it is common to treat intentions as if they originate from one individual mind. In OD and process consulting literature, this is called 'visions', which are expected to be articulated clearly in behavioural terms by senior management so 'new ways of working' are clear and non-negotiable (Schein, 2017, p. 328). I have argued earlier in this project that intentions emerge in ongoing conversations. In the narrative, I was inspired by the perspective of complex responsive processes of relating. I was trying to accept that I cannot be in control and, therefore, worked with a less controlling approach than I am accustomed to as a consultant. I shared how I experienced the feelings that arose in me in the meetings. But my frustration about Carl's second outburst expressed how I had expected, but failed, to control his behaviour towards a more positive state. As we all engaged with our experience and expectations in the living present, no one was in control about where the process of engaging would lead us because, even though we anticipated how others would respond, we did not know for sure. So, we can never plan or predict the future with certainty. I am arguing that we all have intentions, and I am not saying that sharing intentions for the future is a wrong way to go, but the way we bring it up influences the patterns of our relating.

Norman critically explores the idea that we can either have or implement a vision into practice from the perspective of complex responsive processes of relating (2012, p. 191). She claims that the implementation of desired changes in an organisation rests on a set of problematic assumptions such as: 'It is possible for those at the centre to develop policies and procedures (forms of simple rules) that are followed by those lower down the structure to produce a uniform output ... It is possible to ensure that the whole system understands such plans through conveying clear messages' (2012, pp. 193–194). Norman also lists how we usually explain why implementation fails: 'The leaders have not planned it right. The plan was not communicated properly ... Staff were resistant to change, exhibiting poor attitudes or "did not care"' (2012, p. 194). It might be tempting to blame Carl for not planning and communicating right, which he even did himself, or the managers for resistance or poor attitude. Carl's effort to present a clear vision, unfortunately, made us dependent on him to reveal more of the vision and made me respond with planning activities that ironically constrained the managers from acting further. His vision of local cohesion made him appear as a person who had access to something that the rest of us did not. Mowles writes critically about visions in organisational work. 'It seems to me that vision is a highly abstract quasi-religious concept that reinforces the idea of leader as charismatic individual and ascribes to them semi-mystical powers' (2011, p. 117). Mowles describes how this is 'also an appeal to conformity and obedience. Visions have disciplinary power' (2011, p.

118). We all acted as if Carl possessed a vision, and the managers and I became dependent on Carl to reveal more of the vision which supported a pattern with him in a more powerful position but also constrained the managers from acting further on local cohesion where we, the managers and I, continually looked at Carl to seek approval for whether what we were doing was in accordance with his vision.

Power in the narrative

My learning set has continually remarked how they have found that the power relations are important for understanding the narrative. They have drawn attention to how I seemed particularly eager not to disappoint Carl and turned to the helping position as a process consultant when he expressed his disappointment. And when I brought the pattern of disappointment up with the group, I sought his approval, and we all felt a release of tension when Carl acknowledged that it was important to discuss. Once events started to become unclear in terms of how the group was going to work together and whether Carl was to decide the meaning of local cohesion, anxiety arose, and emotions intensified. To avoid this, I turned to safer grounds as a supporting and helping consultant which distracted us from discussing our power relations. I brought the patterns of disappointment up for discussion in the group, but I did not bring up my frustration over the recurrence of disappointment. In hindsight, I think this was because the emotions were more intense in the latter, and I was worried about how this might lead to a conflict that involved Carl and me. My learning set also wondered how power might have influenced how I felt he was disappointed with us whereas I could have been disappointed with him instead, and I side with Mowles as he argues that it is a characteristic of process consulting that it does not enable discussions of power relations (2009, p. 286). This view is maintained in Bushe's recent development of process consulting since he incorporates the appreciative positive way to converse and thereby avoids discussions about power because these might lead to conflict, which is regarded as dysfunctional. Since the aim is to help the clients, one might argue that it supports the client's existing position of power, and this might be a reason why clients find process consulting valuable. But of course, this also constrains what we might reflect upon.

I agree with my learning set that to understand what happened in the narrative it is also important to consider power relations and how we were dependent on each other, how we enabled and constrained each other, and how this played out as patterns of relating. This makes me curious about how power can be viewed as a matter of the different relative needs that

Summing up on differences

The perspective of complex responsive processes of relating draws attention to what we are doing in the living present, which involves power relations, our history of local cohesion in the narrative, and why it turned out to be difficult. Although we had agreed to work together in a way in which we would reflect on what we were doing and why we were doing it, we slipped into the habits of planning, implementing, and instilling positive attitudes in others when Carl was under pressure from the board. Stacey presents this as a causality, which I find is an underlying assumption behind process consulting:

> There is an implicitly assumed theory of efficient causality which holds out the promise that *if* a manager uses the tool properly, *then* an improved outcome will be realized. It is in this sense that we can speak of them as the tools and techniques of analytical, technical, calculative or instrument rationality (2012, p. 40 italics in original).

I find that the instrumentalisation with tools, models, and prescriptions relieves us from the anxiety about what to do when we encounter uncertainty and strong emotions. Mowles argues that instrumentalisation is a tendency in contemporary management literature and that one way to think of it is that it enables us to act in situations that seem impossible to act upon and thereby offers hope (Mowles, 2015, p. 48). In the narrative, I was inspired by the perspective of complex responsive processes of relating as I paid attention to my emotions as part of a relational pattern and shared my experience as a participant. But I was also acting in accordance with the social object of process consulting when I tried to use my emotional experience to create a positive atmosphere. In a sense, I was trying to use the perspective of complex responsive processes of relating as a tool within instrumental rationality. When our interactions became conflictual, I began to plan how the organisation could have more local cohesion, as if I could slip in and out of a complexity approach.

Complex responsive processes of relating as a new model of consulting?

I have often heard statements like the following in my work: 'We should bring in more complexity to understand the problem' or 'we need to reduce complexity'. These imply that there can be more or less complexity. But since human interaction is complex in itself, it is not possible to reduce or add complexity. Any attempt to reduce complexity with grids or models might ironically confuse what we are talking about because we need to pay attention to that element as well. So, when we started to plan for more local cohesion in the narrative, I argue that we confused things further because it did not allow us to discuss our intentions and what we were doing. This is the case particularly because the perspective of complex responsive processes of relating is a way to think about what we are doing and not a method to be applied or some way to control complexity.

I strongly relate to the urge to control complexity within human interaction. In Project 1, I described how I had written a book and coined complexity competencies as individual skills to deal with complexity (Larsen & Gregersen, 2017). Looking back, I must admit that when I started on this DMan, I was set on confirming and developing what I had already written: that individual skills were the answer to handle and overcome complexity. Wheatley takes this a step further when she claims that leaders with special abilities can understand the full complexity of issues in a system (2011). Bushe argues likewise that with specific skills we can 'clear the mush' and talk easily and honestly about what is really on our mind (2010, p. 18). But as I have explored my practice in this thesis and engaged with literature, particularly the views on the individual as socially formed by Elias and Mead, I have realised that I have been embedded in a dominant way of thinking that privileged the individual. So, instead of thinking that individual skills would solve the problems I have encountered, I have come to think that this way of thinking is part of the problems I experience in my practice as a consultant.

The authors above rely on an instrumental rationality where skills can be acquired and applied across contexts. Others have applied this rationality to reduce, separate, or control complexity within human interaction in a variety of ways. Lüscher argues that complex problems can be fenced and transformed into dilemmas to be dealt with through steps guided by consultants (2012). She draws on Quinn's idea of a 'competing values framework', claiming that managers are more effective when they actively choose between competing values such as stability and flexibility (Denison, Hooijberg & Quinn, 1995). Snowden (2005) divides problems into complicated and complex ones and assigns different strategies to deal with each area, which Bushe also uses in his work to decide which tools to apply to which problems (Bushe & Marshak, 2016, p. 414). The authors above use some of the same words as the perspective of complex responsive processes of relating but use them in the context of systems thinking, which can be confusing. In my understanding of the perspective of complex responsive processes of relating, I will critique these attempts to reduce, separate, or control complexity. I do so because humans or organisations are not systems that anyone can stand outside of with consultants as neutral autonomous individuals without an individual history or specific relationships.

To be fair to the authors above, the position of the consultant is incorporated to varying degrees as some draw specifically on social constructionism and second-order systemic thinking claiming that no one can stand outside a socially constructed reality. Schein argues that the consultant should take the position of an anthropologist to see the organisational culture from a native point of view to change dysfunctional elements but only vaguely comments that consultants should deploy skills from family therapists in the approach to 'human systems' (2006, p. 299). It is unclear how consultants are supposed to decide what will be the right tool in a given situation, and he does not describe how their own position affects this. Bushe takes issue with this and argues that 'OD practitioners need to be aware of their own immersion in the organization and reflexively consider what meanings they are creating and what narratives their actions are privileging and marginalizing' (Bushe & Marshak, 2016, p. 410). Despite these differences regarding the extent to which they view the consultant as a participant, they all recommend tools and models as known from instrumental rationality (Stacey, 2012, p. 47). In sum, I argue that the above authors overlook, first, that consultants are specific individuals with their own experience and assumptions and, second, how this affects the choices they make with clients.

There is another important distinction to be made between the approaches I have been inspired by earlier and the perspective of complex responsive processes of relating which relates to my experience of responsibility in the narrative. I mentioned earlier how Schein emphasised that the helping position is one that avoids blaming the consultant (Schein, 1995, p. 16). From a participatory approach, we all have responsibility for what happens because our gestures affect others and we are, therefore, responsible whether we wish this or not. So, to claim, like Schein, that consultants should avoid blame seems like a strategic manoeuvre. In the narrative, I had changed my way of working and did not want to avoid blame as I previously would have sought to. I found myself wanting to share the narrative with Carl and the managers because we had built mutual trust in our relationship and I was afraid they would feel betrayed if I were to publish something that they did not like. Since Carl, the managers, and their subordinates knew I was doing this research and would probably read the thesis, I felt I had to show my work to them before publishing as others could read it and might identify them. Although they might agree with what I write, they might not want people in their organisation to have access to it.

So, I decided to share the narrative and sent it to Carl before sending it to the managers since he was the contract holder. It took three weeks before Carl responded, and I found myself emotionally affected by this. I fantasised that he was angry and felt betrayed. It turned out he had just been busy. He wrote that he found the narrative very interesting and it was fine to send it to the managers, so we could meet and discuss it, and eventually publish it in my thesis. He only had a few suggestions regarding anonymisation, which I figured would be manageable to negotiate.

Discussing the narrative with the managers

When we met, Carl started by saying that my project had helped him to see how he affected others. One of the managers added that she had found it comforting to read my detailed account of my doubts and insecurity, which she found were honest and resonant with her own experience in her everyday work. We discussed how we had been able to stay in complex and emotionally difficult situations longer than usual, how this had been valuable, and how they rarely found opportunities to have these kinds of reflections and discussions. They found that explanations like poor leadership or resistance to change were common but thin explanations. They resonated with the descriptions in this project that involved identity as well as negative feelings like anxiety, disappointment, and shame. Our practice was a continual struggle rather than a state we could reach as described in literature on 'high-performance teams' which they had struggled to achieve in earlier leadership development projects (Smith & Katzenbach, 1994). Earlier, they had felt they had to act in a more 'professional way' where it felt wrong to reveal negative feelings and where they were not reflecting on what they or others were doing and why they were doing it. They also explained that they had been able to discuss the pattern of disappointment in the days after the fourth meeting, so even though the pattern had recurred, it had also changed, which enabled them to continue the conversation.

Towards the end of our meeting, they asked if they could hire me again and if I could lead a workshop where all their managers could read my projects and discuss my reflections. When they gave their approval for the publication of the narrative and expressed that my work and our discussions were valuable, I felt affirmed and intensely relieved.

When I tried to make sense of the events with my learning set, they paid attention to my feelings of relief and remarked how important it seemed for me to impress Carl and the managers. They also raised a question about my eagerness to work differently in this narrative as compared to the narrative in Project 2. Was that also to impress them and the rest of the DMan community? Was I, again, orchestrating an effort to impress an audience? I noticed that I was somewhat defensive about their questions, but the reflections brought my attention to my first project and the repeated pattern of my need to impress in Project 2. So, although I am still ambiguous, I have concluded that performing to control other people's reactions towards me to impress them is truly animating not only for me but also for understanding consultancy in organisational development in general. My ambiguity about engaging with this idea is because I did not act as I did in the narrative just to impress, but also to help Carl and the managers. But the ambiguity is surely also because admitting to myself and being honest about how I perform to impress, changes the impression I am having on others. In that sense, I lose control of the impression I am making, which feels revealing and is anxiety-provoking for me. This has made me interested in the following question: Why and how do we perform to make others think positively about us, and what impact does this have in consultancy in organisational development?

Performing to impress

When I started the DMan, I was struck by the persuasive argument that if we are to take unpredictability seriously, we must regard organisational life as the interweaving of intentions, which means that consultants cannot predict or guarantee that things will develop to the positive. In this sense, consultants who make transformational promises are over-promising (Mowles, 2009, p. 292), which I argue will inevitably lead to disappointment. Mowles and Stacey claim that common responses to unpredictability are intensive efforts to avoid being blamed and feeling incompetent (2016, p. 96).

As I have written earlier, my interaction with people is gradually changing, and I am exploring ways to act as a consultant without being an expert who impresses others through strategic plans, personality profiles, models, and concepts. In Project 2, I experimented with a less controlling way of working. This led me to be disappointed, but instead of my habitual response of suppressing it, I engaged with the feelings, which allowed me to explore further what was important both to me and to others. In the narrative in this project, I began to move away from being affirmed as I drew attention to patterns of disappointment. In both projects, I oscillated between a need to be affirmed and gaining detachment from it, allowing me to explore how affirmation affected what we were doing. As another small example from my practice, I have noticed how I used to enjoy the common practice of people clapping when I have given a talk or conducted a workshop. Lately, this practice has made me reflect on what the clapping might express. People might be pleased with my performance, but they might also respond to my need to be affirmed, to expected patterns of relating, power relations, or something completely different. I experience that consultants, although claiming to be neutral experts who are helping clients to find their own solutions, need recognition and have intentions of their own which affect their work. Therefore, I will explore how I can understand my interactions as a consultant in organisational development as a performance trying to impress others to think positively about myself.

Human interaction as performances intended to impress others is described by the sociologist Goffman (1959), and I will consult his original ideas and explore the development in later theories on 'impression management' afterwards.

Goffman and the art of impression management in everyday life

Goffman is located in the tradition of ethnomethodology and draws on a dramaturgical metaphor to describe behaviour as performance and argues that individuals are always trying to control the impression they make on others (1959, p. 26). He quotes the American pragmatist William James and argues that our performance is always in relation to an audience. This is, to ideas about who one think may be listening and watching. Any man 'has as many different social selves as there are distinct *groups* of persons about whose opinion he cares' (ibid, p. 57 italics in original).

He describes human interactions as a 'working consensus' where everybody has an interest in maintaining norms as mutual agreements about how we relate to each other (ibid, p. 21). If we do not maintain and act in accordance with norms, we risk disrupting our interaction with others, which might cause embarrassment and what he has described as 'losing face' (1959, p. 24, 1967, p. 5). He uses the term 'face' to describe the positive social value a person wants others to have of oneself. The individual losing face will feel shame, and others will feel ill at ease about it. He argues that the immediate response from everybody involved is to avoid these disruptions and thereby try not only to save our face but also avoid that others lose theirs (1967, p. 9). Taking Goffman's insights to organisational development would mean that we always respond to norms and expectations about how managers and consultants are competent in their work to keep a positive social value and avoid embarrassment (1959, p. 43). A great number of authors have taken up his ideas about 'impression management' in management and consultancy, and I will outline their contributions briefly before I delve into how I might use these ideas to understand the narrative further.

Hochschild takes up impression management particularly with regard to emotions in her descriptions about how people adapt to 'feeling rules'. She quotes Goffman to say that 'rules seem to govern how people work to feel in ways "appropriate to the situation"' (Hochschild, 1979, p. 552). Balkan and Soran also describe emotions and focus on how emotional expressions correspond to impression management 'tactics' that are used by employees (2013). The management of impressions in the above is seen as unconscious attunement or conscious tactics to manage emotions and the impression they make on others. They both focus on the submissive character of expectations, rules, and norms on the individual. This is elaborated further within critical management approach in the seminal article by Alvesson and Willmott (2002) in which 'employees are enjoined to develop self-images and work orientations that are deemed congruent with managerially defined objectives' (ibid, p. 619). The submission required by employees is not only a deliberate action from the manager but is discursively embedded, as Alvesson and Willmott illustrate in an example where managers are persuaded to have a particular responsibility to be positive towards change (ibid, p. 632). Hodgson shares this focus in his work on how project managers must submit to the conduct expected and 'put on a professional performance' to gain legitimacy in their role (2005, p. 53). All the above have a focus on submission and adaptation imposed on employees either by managers or from a broader discursive perspective. I find this focus on expectations, rules, and norms as co-created patterns of relating that form professional identity valuable to understand the narrative. As a short example from the narrative, I tried to live up to expectations when I slipped into supporting Carl's request to engineer the future. This was in line with orthodox ideas about strategic planning that, according to Clegg et al. (2004), rely on the notion that management seeks to control the organisation through plans and strategies (ibid, p. 21).

To broaden the perspective on impression management within consultancy, I have come across other authors who have turned the tables and argue that consultants are the ones managing the relationship as they manage the impression they make on clients. Clark writes that consultants perform to control the client (1995, p. 100) and that 'successful consultancy is essentially about relationship management' (ibid, p. 17). Smith argues that consultants basically manage the client-relation by giving the impression that they bring value to clients without arguing, but simply implying, that helping the client to do what they want is valuable to the client (ibid, p. 62). Kristensen takes the argument further and concludes that consultants within OD traditions are not creating more effective organisations but are only giving the impression that they do (2006, p. 264).

I find that the literature on impression management I have brought in helps to understand how I tried to impress Carl, the managers, and my research community. But I was not the only one being busy to impress others. Carl was trying to control the future to leave the impression with the board that he was creating a clear direction for the organisation. The managers were trying to leave the impression on Carl that they were trying to do what he wanted. With regard to my position, I will argue, with words from Smith, that we were all under the influence of 'collectively held definitions of what kind of social actors consultants are in relation to other actors, their characteristics, attributes and abilities, the roles they play as well as the value of their activities and attributes' (2008, p. 52). In this project, I have pointed specifically to process consulting, but other social objects such as 'management' and 'board' would be relevant as well but outside the scope of this thesis.

In sum, I argue that we were all active actors with intentions that were conditioned by our past experiences and expectations, which developed as they interweaved. So, we were not only passively submitted to broader patterns within consultancy and management, because at the same time, we were intentionally experimenting with new ways of working and thereby changing our work together. It was an interplay of intentions, and I find that whereas Goffman describes existing norms in our relating and how we respond to these norms, Mead extends this understanding as he describes that norms are to be understood as patterns in our gesturing as we interact with each other but also how our actions change these norms over time (Baldwin, 1988, p. 51; Curtis, 2018, pp. 72–73). Curtis elaborates on Goffman's term 'working consensus' to go beyond this as a response to fixed norms. He coined this 'functional collusion' by which he means both a conscious agreement and unconscious patterns of relating that incorporates habits, social objects, and our relations to each other (2018, p. 58).

Functional collusion in the narrative

In the narrative, 'functional collusion' involves the interactions between all of us before and after our meetings and includes our expectations, the development from one meeting to the next, and our reflections as we discussed the narrative later. These collusions stabilise the ways we respond to each other and allow us to move on together. 'Such collusion has the function of giving certainty and predictability to those colluding and reduces their anxiety' (Curtis, 2018, p. 56). This explains how there was simultaneously change and stability in the narrative. Just because I brought our attention to a pattern of disappointment, it did not disappear, and thereby it stayed the same. At the same time, it enabled a change that allowed them to continue discussions about disappointment, as they explained when we met and discussed this narrative. When I drew attention to disappointment as a pattern of relating, I challenged the 'functional collusion' and I could have kept doing it, but that would have challenged my power relation with Carl with the risk of exclusion. Alvesson and Willmott (2002) would probably argue that my participation was a way to perpetuate existing power relationships, particularly as I was contracted by the top manager and my success in the change process would be to support this power structure which would, ironically for a person in the business of change consultancy, keep things the same. In contrast, Kristensen would probably argue that I skillfully managed to give them the impression that my work was valuable and lured them into hiring me again (Kristensen, 2006, pp. 238–239).

I am not arguing that we should not or cannot manage the impressions we leave with each other; neither am I naïvely suggesting that we can 'clear the mush' and interact as if there are no differences in our intentions or power differentials present as Bushe claims (2010). I argue that we are all reflexive individuals with the potential to reflect on what we are doing and why we are doing it together to find possibilities to move on together. Curtis sees colluding as functional because it allows us to relate to each other and continue our conversations. He finds that consultancy within organisational development is preoccupied with change and should probably pay more attention to why things stay the same. This might help us to understand more about what is important to people.

I find that Curtis's understanding of 'functional collusion' incorporates Goffman's view on impression management and Mead's perspective on social relating in the living present and offers a way to understand colluding that we become aware of. I wrote that, at the beginning of my work with the managers, I found it almost too easy and comfortable to work with less preplanning. My decision to collude with the ideas about planning the future and keeping a positive atmosphere was not conscious. I felt I was swaying in the wind, agreeing on whatever the different people needed. I was trying to balance the needs of the group while creating a positive atmosphere with the managers and the outcome-designing approach that Carl suggested, particularly when Carl, from his position of power, expressed it with strong emotions. It became so difficult for me then that I unconsciously slipped back to performing in the role of a process consultant to lower the anxiety and avoid exclusion.

Responsibility when we cannot predict what happens

Questioning our functional colluding might make people anxious and cause harm, and I am not suggesting that this is what consultants should be doing without great caution. If we consider the mutual affirmation in Project 2 as a functional collusion, it allowed us to question the function of this in the aftermath of the meeting, which helped us to learn from it. But no one can predict what happens when colluding is questioned; in similar situations, we might cause too much confusion and anxiety and disrupt the continuity of our conversations. This calls for a contextual and sensitive approach to what we are doing together because, although we do not know how our actions influence others, we still have the responsibility to take others seriously and continuously pay attention to how our actions affect others. This concerns both the publication of the narrative and my work with people in general since the nature of my work involves reflections that might cause harm. I expect to delve into ethics further in Project 4.

When I engaged in the planning to implement local cohesion, I tried to live up to Carl's expectations and help him in his efforts. But it also deflected a discussion about what was important in the group: that is, why local cohesion was difficult and what that might tell us. Instead, I found myself with a strong need to impress, a responsibility to help, and a need to create a positive atmosphere. Gradually, I am paying more attention to how my and others' impression management and pursuit of affirmation affects what we are doing together, and I will continue my work to explore this, particularly in relation to power and what consultants are supposed to do. Mowles suggests that the role of a consultant 'is to work with groups of managers or leaders to become more detached about their involvement in organizational life, to help them pay attention to what is most closely concerning them' (2011, p. 253). I am not arguing that functional collusions involving structured methods are wrong in themselves. And I am not arguing that we can or should relate without affirming each other. It might be both helpful and honest to affirm, recognise, and point out strengths, but if it is dogmatic, it becomes blind like any other generic tool or approach.

Summing up my argument so far

The generalisable claims I make in my research so far are summed up here.

I claim that consultants and managers are often affirmed when they can present themselves to be in control of future outcomes and the mindset of others. I argue that the future is uncertain, and when we try to control it, disappointment will inevitably arise at some point. Failure to control or even a lack of affirmation involves strong emotional reactions experienced as threats to the continuity of the relationship and one's identity. I argue that the continual affirmation of people and highlighting of success can lead to an unrealistic sense of individual responsibility, where we blame ourselves for failure and feel affirmed for events that we are not responsible for nor in control of (Brinkmann, 2017; Ehrenreich, 2010). I regard this as an underlying pattern in Western societies about wanting to stand out as extraordinary individuals (Elias, 2001, pp. 141–142), and I find that consultants and managers respond to this by trying to impress others in order to be affirmed. Since there is a strong preference in current consultancy-practice within organisational development only to focus on positive emotions (Maxton & Bushe, 2018), the engagement in feelings like disappointment and shame is avoided, also because it is a threat to the identity of the consultant. This is important because the discussion of the consultant's motives challenges OD perspectives where the consultant's need for affirmation is often neglected. I argue that these patterns of relating can be seen as functional colluding, which is stabilising but also hinders important reflections about what we are doing together. I am paying attention to the above, and this causes my practice to change. I have grown increasingly curious about the connection between power and affirmation and how affirmation from Carl seemed more important to me, as if my reflexive stance was constrained when there was a power struggle and I risked a lack of affirmation or perhaps even exclusion.

Further explorations

I am striving to develop a practice as a consultant in organisational development that involves drawing attention to emotions and how they express patterns of relating, and what we might learn from this. I am not aspiring for a practice with complete detachment from the need to be affirmed, nor do I consider that this is possible. I am rather paying attention to when and why I and others perform to impress and gain affirmation and how this might be connected to power. Since I am challenging the idea that consultants should help managers achieve their goals by creating a positive attitude in others, I am curious to explore what I think consultants should be doing instead. Calling out how we collude with each other might disrupt the existing power structure, arouse feelings of anxiety, and be painful for people, so I am interested in exploring the ethics in consultancy.

Project 4: Power, identity, and ethics in consultancy

In my work as a consultant, I have identified how the need to be positively affirmed is important to me. In the course of this research, I have found that the tendency to manage the impression one makes on others to make them think positively about oneself resonates with my learning set, clients and consultants, and literature I have consulted so far. This need to be positively affirmed is due partly to the nature of my employment as a self-employed consultant—influenced by the imperative to acquire clients, endlessly establish new relationships, and continuously prove one's worth. In other words, performing to impress others is a generalisable pattern, but for personal and professional reasons it may be amplified in my case. So, before I present the last narrative in this thesis, I will explore how the pressure to perform as a management consultant is described more generally (Czarniawska & Mazza, 2003; Smith, 2008; Stein, 2017; Sturdy, 1997; Sturdy, Schwarz & Spicer, 2006). My aim in this short introduction is not to discuss their differences or the differences between their practices and mine. Rather, in order to make the case that my experience has wider implications beyond my specific situation, I aim to present similarities regarding pressures that management consultants more generally are exposed to.

Numerous authors argue that consultants operate in liminal spaces where regular routines are suspended resulting in a fluid and largely unstructured space (Czarniawska & Mazza, 2003, p. 267; Stein, 2018a, p. 282; Sturdy et al., 2006, p. 932). Managers expect consultants to secure a sense of control in the liminal space (Sturdy, 1997, p. 397) yet are simultaneously under pressure to avoid threatening the manager's image of being in control (Sturdy, 1997, p. 404). Consultants are often seen as 'magical outsiders' who can challenge client's assumptions and do things insiders cannot do (Smith, 2008, p. 60) but at the same time need to act as insiders as they engage in social relationships and display an understanding of the nature of the client's work (Stein, 2017, p. 82). They might even face expectations to be geniuses with special powers (Czarniawska & Mazza, 2003, p. 280). I resonate with this as I was presented once, to my dismay, as an Olympic champion of conflict solving. Stein argues that consultants are often hired to speed up processes and staff; that they are 'selling speed' which in turn creates a sense of urgency within the consultants themselves (Stein, 2018b, p. 104). Consultants are expected to organise changes for others (Czarniawska & Mazza, 2003, p. 285) and are not expected to have objectives of their own or to undergo change themselves (ibid, pp. 275–278). 'They need to be more than flexible—they need to be pliable' (ibid, p. 277). Serious illnesses such as stomach ulcers, stress-related nervous breakdown, and heart attacks are reported as reactions to this pressure (Stein, 2018b, p. 104).

Sturdy claims that consultancy is a 'high pressure existence … It is often a highly competitive, hierarchical, individualistic and sometimes insecure work environment' (1997, pp. 406–407). Work in this environment might be profoundly unsettling (Sturdy et al., 2006, p. 932). Sturdy argues that literature mostly focuses on managers' 'human angst, insecurity, doubt and frailty' (1997, p. 392), whereas consultants 'tend to be portrayed as confident and "in control"' (ibid, p. 405). He claims, however, that consultants are subjected to 'similar pressures and uncertainties' as the managers (ibid, p. 390). Additionally, consultants are easily subjected to blame and scapegoating if things go wrong (Alvesson, 2001, p. 869; Clark, 1995, p. 14; Sturdy, 1997, p. 404).

The literature cited above suggests that this pressure to perform is a general pattern for consultants. This is the highly generalisable backdrop of my need to impress others. Being positively affirmed used to be an Archimedean point to me, and still is, to some extent, but my research has allowed me to take a more detached view of my need for affirmation. After inquiring into the pressure to impress from a relational perspective, rather than merely as an individual need, power and ethics have emerged as themes in the last project. I will explore this further in a narrative that describes my work in a non-profit organisation for mentally disabled children.

Narrative: My stand as a consultant

My first visit to this organisation was in 2017, where I met with the manager John to plan a strategy seminar for all the managers in the organisation. John showed me around and was warmly greeted and hugged by several of the children we met. He appeared very charismatic to me as he told me how the organisation had been founded 10 years earlier by a group of parents who wanted him to start a boarding school for their children. These parents were unhappy about the government schools, so they founded the organisation, took positions as board members, and hired John. They seemed to have unconditional trust in John's leadership, which was easy for me to understand as he animatedly told me about the organisation's achievements and ambitions. He wanted to change society's attitudes so that children could participate in the broader community and feel like equals. This enthusiastic approach proved appealing to other parents, and the school grew in size. They had expanded with new departments such as a local shop, a café, a gardening business, and housing units where the children with special needs could work and live after finishing school. The organisation reached a total of 100 employees, which led to a separation into two organisations, the original 'boarding school' and a housing and occupational department called 'the foundation'. John had established a practice where students from 'the school' were encouraged to go to the foundation. Peter, who had been an employee since the organisation was founded, was promoted to CEO for the school and John became CEO of the foundation. For legal reasons, the original board was also formally separated into two, and although the same members sat in both boards, they had two different board members as their chairs.

After the seminar in 2017, I was continually hired by both management teams to reflect on their work together with them in monthly meetings. At one of these meetings in late 2018, Peter said he favoured concentrating on the boarding school's tasks for a while instead of meeting with both management teams and me. John disagreed with this, but he could not persuade Peter. John continued to hire me to work with him and his two managers in the foundation. In the period of these meetings, they experienced a decreased flow of students from the school which gave rise among them to a critique of the school.

In spring 2019, John and Peter asked me to lead a two-day seminar for boards and management teams to discuss the strategy for both organisations and to plan and facilitate a presentation of the strategy to all the staff on an awayday one week later.

Planning the board seminar

I agreed and met with John, Peter, and the two chairs to plan the seminar. The chairs told me that the organisation needed to work as one movement rather than two organisations. Due to my work in Project 3, I paid greater attention to power relations, and I commented that they were actually two organisations and suggested that we explore how they were dependent on each other. Both chairs promptly rejected the idea of exploring this and insisted that we focus on the need to develop as one movement. I briefly introduced Elias's ideas about power and interdependency and suggested that reflecting on the dependencies between the school and the foundation might be helpful, especially because the chairs as well as John and Peter formally were equals and thereby dependent on each other to work as one movement.

The chairs eagerly responded that loyalty towards the overall values and purpose had absolute primacy and that this loyalty overruled any interest that might serve only the school or the foundation. Their emphasis on values seemed automated and mantra-like. John and Peter were quiet. I kept thinking that their power relations were relevant to discuss but that my invitation to do so had been rejected. So, I planned the seminar in a rather conventional way to consist of presentations of their current developmental projects, discussing ideas for new initiatives and reflections about how to involve the staff in the continual development of the strategy. The process would then include the board seminar, the awayday for all staff one week later and a planning meeting with the managers in between.

The board seminar

The seminar progressed as planned for the first half day. But as soon as I initiated the discussion about how the organisations could develop further, John stood up and gave a longer speech about how the school should actively counsel students to start in the foundation. Peter replied that he found himself doing exactly that, but still respecting the law that stated that counselling at schools should be independent of interests other than those of the students. John sat uneasily in his chair and responded in a loud and clear voice that it was in the interest of the students to go to the foundation and that the law was nowhere as clear-cut as Peter was suggesting. Silence followed. I was a bit shocked by how aggressively John came across. I suggested that we might consult the law. This was rapidly followed by a series of statements from board members that were supportive of John's perspective. Their support seemed coordinated to me, and their unity made me withdraw from pursuing my suggestion. I ended the day with an uncomfortable sense that Peter was isolated and seen by the rest as disloyal to the overall purpose of the movement. I intuitively agreed with Peter's view on the law but figured that if I raised the question of legality, it might lead to further exclusion of Peter and perhaps exclude myself too. So, although I felt an urge to support Peter, I felt unable to act and decided to go on with the planned programme. Peter kept a low profile for the rest of the seminar. Towards the end of the seminar, the boards decided that they wanted the organisations to work more closely and to involve the staff in these endeavours on the awayday the week after.

Two days later, I met with both management teams to discuss my plan for the awayday. Peter objected in a quiet way about a task where the boards had wanted the staff to work on how they could counsel the students to go to the foundation. He remained sceptical about whether this was legal. This created another awkward silence. I had been working with them for years and had experienced intense disagreements but never such a tense and stuck atmosphere as the one that arose. I shared how I experienced the silence and said I felt it was centred around John and Peter. I asked if others could recognise what I was saying and what these feelings might express. Everyone nodded, and one manager said it was as if there were an elephant in the room that no one had commented on until now. Peter said he agreed but did not know how to move on from here. John ostentatiously repeated it was a task that the board wanted, so there was no more to discuss. I felt I had become part of a power-play between the two. We ended the meeting shortly after.

Peter called me the following day. He felt John had orchestrated the whole process and persuaded the boards to find ways to send students to the foundation. I said that one way to look at it might be that John was dependent on the school to send students to the foundation and he had managed to put pressure on Peter to make this happen. Peter agreed and said that the board seminar had made him feel naïve and painfully aware that he was in a game of power. He was considering how to play this game but felt constrained and unable to act without risking accusations of disloyalty and perhaps exclusion. I said I was trying to focus on the day for the staff and that the board had explicitly asked to work with the counselling task, so I felt I had to go on with this. I added that I felt our reflections were important, but that having the conversation without John made me feel disloyal. He understood my position and did not expect me to choose sides. He just needed to talk to someone who might understand his frustration. I felt uncomfortable about the situation.

I realised that I was forced to choose sides and, although I sympathised with Peter's argument about the law, I was about to take John's side. I was puzzled about why this was so when I disagreed with him. I believe it was because I was aware of

John's strong relational history with the board and felt I could not raise the issue with John without facing exclusion whereby I would be cut off from any further intervention. And besides, wasn't my role as a consultant to support what the two chairs wanted for the organisation? At seminars and awaydays, I am used to thinking of myself as a helper to convey the clients' wishes and facilitate processes that allow the employees to explore and make sense of these wishes to reach consensus in a harmonious atmosphere. I am usually competent at bringing this about, and I am affirmed for succeeding to do so. I had a diffuse bodily sensation of unease and restlessness, which I related to an ethical responsibility that reached beyond leaving or facilitating what those in formal power wanted. But I did not know what to do. I felt constrained and guilty for not insisting on raising my voice about it. This has led me to think about similar experiences in the past, and I realise that if I have experienced clients as unethical, I have found discrete ways to terminate the relationship as I did when I was a manager as described in Project 1. But my explorations in Project 3 have made me take seriously the experience that there is something wrong and stay with that experience.

The day for all of staff

The day started as planned with the board members presenting the history of the organisation. At the first break, I overheard two recent members of the boards talking to each other about how Peter had contacted a lawyer and had written to both boards and management teams the evening before about it. The lawyer had made it clear that counselling should be free of any interests other than the students', so the school could not counsel towards the foundation. And further, as the board members sat in both boards, they had a financial motive to counsel towards the foundation which was illegal. The lawyer clearly stated that the boards should be completely separated with different members in each. The new board members were nervous. They did not want to be part of any illegal activities. Privately I felt a sting of admiration for Peter. He had found a way to voice his concern. But I was also worried about whether he would be fired, and my concern was strengthened when I noticed how John was furiously engaged in private conversations with different board members. The other managers and the board members looked perplexed or paralysed. I carried on with the programme, and although no one spoke to me about it, I was sure that the employees noticed the tension.

I did not have further appointments with either John or Peter after this. While driving home, I was determined to stop working for them. I had facilitated the days as requested, but I felt like a puppet on a string, initially with John as the puppeteer, superseded by Peter. I sympathised with both of them for their dedication to improving the lives of mentally disabled children but felt it had turned into a primitive battle of egos. I could not understand why they were not able to discuss their disagreements in a civilised manner. After a week, I decided to write an email to John and Peter suggesting that the three of us should meet. I wrote that I sympathised strongly with their purpose as an organisation and that I liked and respected them both, but that their struggles were difficult for me to witness because I found them counterproductive to their wish to help mentally disabled people. By sending it, I feared they might think of my mail as untimely and be angry with me. They replied separately that they appreciated my initiative but felt that further dialogue with the other would not solve anything. Their response made me sad.

A few weeks later, John asked me to continue our monthly meetings to reflect on their leadership with him and his managers throughout 2019. My initial thought was to turn him down. But I was reminded of the events in Project 1 where I still feel guilty for quietly resigning instead of standing up for what I believed was right for the organisation and the mentally disabled children. After careful consideration, I began to think of it as a possibility to keep working with the messy stuff, and that this might be more helpful for the children instead of running away. Besides, as a self-employed consultant, I also need work. Eventually, I agreed to continue our work.

I learned how Peter had gotten his way so that the two boards were formally and practically separated. When I questioned John and the managers in the foundation about how they felt about this, John decisively said it was best forgotten and time to look forward. The two other managers in the foundation expressed a sense of loss, though. I insisted on exploring this and drew on a DMan colleague's work on loss in organisational life where she explored what could be learned from feelings of loss (Askeland, 2019). This enabled a discussion of a shared sadness about how the separation had taken place. It brought hope to my aspiration that they could, in time, reengage in conversations with Peter and the school. This was one among several instances where I found myself making more risky gestures. I have openly challenged John and reflected on how his passionate behaviour might be experienced as intimidating and make others withdraw, because I have observed this with others, and this is also how he affects me. To my surprise, he did not act defensively or aggressively but engaged with curiosity in explorations about how he might affect others. Another risky gesture was my decision to write this narrative because both John and Peter knew I was doing research, and they would definitely read my work. I had a notion of betrayal by writing about them without their knowing. I did not know how to deal with this at the time, but I knew that I would have to at some point.

Initial reflections

One might argue that from the perspective of process consulting, as described in Project 3, I had successfully managed to position myself as a helper and thereby avoided being blamed by both John and Peter. John had hired me again. Peter also attended an open workshop I had held after the events in the narrative. According to critical perspectives on process consulting, also mentioned in Project 3 (Clark, 1995; Kristensen, 2006; Smith, 2008), I managed the relationships with the client by appearing useful. Also, from a commercial perspective, I could be seen as successful as I was hired again by John. I did not feel successful, though. The two organisations were not working well together anymore, and I feared this would have consequences for the mentally disabled people they were trying to help. Later on, I came to know that Peter had gotten a new job and had left the school. This made me sad but also relieved because it was a deadlock as long as they were unable to work together. I was disappointed that John and Peter could not find a novel way around their conflict or at least talk about it.

One immediate response from my learning set upon reading the narrative was that, in contrast to the narratives in Projects 2 and 3, I was paying more attention to why John and Peter acted as they did and the consequences for the children than worrying about them affirming me. But the subsequent discussion with the learning set also made me realise I was making negative judgments about John and Peter as being political, which distracted me from working out how to get involved in the politics myself. So, while I might be worrying less about recognition for myself, my withdrawal from games of power might not support the children's needs. I realise that my habitual wish to withdraw from conflict and power struggles is founded in my assumptions about consultancy. In Project 3, I argued that process consulting and dialogic OD cover over power relations whereas second-order systemic and social constructionist thinking regard it as an unfortunate construction we should avoid (Solso, 2016, p. 188). Fineman (2006, p. 271) points to how appreciative inquiry, which has inspired both process consulting and dialogic OD (Bushe & Marshak, 2015), specifically recommends avoiding problems such as power struggles since they claim that disagreement, conflict, and negative feelings are dysfunctional, created through language, and should be avoided. Although I am critically paying attention to the above in my practice and presented Elias's view on power as interdependencies at the first planning meeting, it did not lead to discussions about conflicting interests. They seemed eager to conclude that we were serving the same cause and that there was no conflict of interests. I found it difficult and uncomfortable to challenge this belief further. With the benefit of hindsight, my intervention with Elias was a very abstract and academic way to ask them to engage with issues of power, which made it difficult for us to engage in the potentially daunting dynamic between them and, in turn, easy for them to dismiss. I must admit I was relieved when the discussion of conflicting interests was off the table, and in that sense, we were all colluding to avoid engaging with power. These reflections have made me realise that I often bring theory into my work with clients. One reason might be that it is a way to make an impression as competent. Another reason might be that referring to theory draws the attention away from my stand, which makes it easier for me to withdraw from discussion and avoid conflict. But it left me unable to voice my concerns more clearly. I was not able to act sufficiently into the political game of power, although I believed it was problematic for the welfare of the children.

This made me curious to explore how I might understand political games of power within consultancy, and I consulted an overview article on power in organisational work (Fleming & Spicer, 2014). The authors argue that politics concern the distribution of goods through the mobilisation of power: 'Power is the capacity to influence other actors with these political interests in mind' (ibid, p. 239). They observe that political activity is typically seen as a nuisance to ordered social action and is considered to be kept at a minimum (ibid, p. 239). I resonate with the latter in my attempts to avoid open manifestations of conflicting interests in my pursuit of affirmation. I am interested in exploring further how political games of power might not be something one can or should avoid, how power might both be 'nasty and backstabbing' but also a force to achieve great things in organisational development (ibid, p. 240). I will explore this in relation to my theme of affirmation and my problems in finding out what was the right thing to do as a consultant. Fleming and Spicer draw on Lukes (2005) who has explored the hidden mechanisms of power which I will consult in the following.

Power

Power is typically defined as a capacity for one person to cause a particular behaviour in another against the latter's will as explained by several authors although this is only the simplest explanation (Fleming & Spicer, 2014, p. 238; Han, 2019, p. 1; Lukes, 2005, p. 12). Lukes calls this the first dimension of power. He argues that power is easy to observe when there is an observable conflict of interests—where A forces B to act in A's interests. However, it is difficult to observe when someone is setting the agenda for what might be discussed. He calls the latter the second dimension of power whereby 'the power to decide what is decided' (ibid, p. 111) is about keeping certain topics on or off an agenda. These two dimensions of power are relevant when there is an observable conflict of interests. Lukes formulates a third dimension to describe the power to prevent conflict of interests from arising in the first place. This is about the power 'to prevent people, to whatever degree, from having grievances by shaping their perceptions, cognitions and preferences in such a way that they accept their role in the existing order of things' (ibid, p. 11). Here, power is also about shaping people's way of seeing the world (ibid, p. 29).

In the narrative, I felt I was suddenly in the middle of a power struggle. But just because I had not noticed it as an open conflict did not mean that there was not a conflict of interests earlier on. I noticed power in the first dimension as an open conflict over interests when John accused Peter of not advising students to go to the foundation. I noticed power in the second dimension at the board seminar where the agenda was influenced to prevent or promote certain topics coming up. I felt unable to act, which is precisely how power is played out in the second dimension. Power in the third dimension in the narrative explains how disagreements were kept out of open discussions altogether through the shaping of desires and beliefs (Lukes, 2005, p. 144). This appeared to me as agreement throughout my first two years with them, but Lukes' theory of power brings attention to how it was political all along; I just did not see it. The tradition of process consulting and second-order systemic thinking stresses that bringing attention to conflicting interests would not be helpful, might amplify or even create conflicts. I was reluctant to engage in conflicting interests because this might have altered the impression I would make as someone who could create a harmonious atmosphere, which blinded me to the political nature of what was going on. I find Lukes helpful for understanding that power was at play, although I did not observe it as a conflict before it was openly expressed at the board seminar. I was not suddenly caught up in a game of power that I should have avoided. The power differentials were there all along, and John's use of force at the board seminar and Peter's mail were overt expressions of the power differentials. Lukes is particularly helpful in explaining the dynamics of power and the manifestations as persuasion, manipulation, coercion, and force in the movement from covert to overt (Lukes, 2005, p. 36).

However, there are also issues in the narrative that Lukes's perspective on power does not explain. This concerns the complexity of how the events played out between us as specific individuals with separate histories and expectations as well as a history together where we continuously affected each other. I disagree with Lukes's sharp separation of people as A's and B's with fixed interests because this assumes that Peter, John, and I had isolated interests that were not affected by how our relations developed. In contrast, I experienced that my conversations with Peter might have encouraged him to rebel against John. Also, I found myself less occupied about whether they would affirm me as events evolved, which led me to challenge John towards the end of the narrative. Lukes does not explain this ongoing development of our relations because his analysis of power is at an abstract level, detached from experience and history. To understand power as embedded in specific practices, I have found the French sociologist Bourdieu helpful, and I will explore his perspective below.

Field, symbolic capital, and habitus in the narrative

Bourdieu stresses the importance of the field in which events take place. A field contains dynamics of power; who is dominated, who dominates, and who defines the principles of domination (Emirbayer & Johnson, 2008, p. 24). A field consists of structures such as the market, competitors, and the history of the field (Bourdieu, 2005, p. 206) that are more lasting than the visible particular individuals (Bourdieu & Wacquant, 1992, pp. 113–114). These structures are of interest for understanding power rather than individuals who are merely expressing positions in the game of power within the field, according to Bourdieu. So, to understand what happened in the narrative requires an interrogation into how we were individuals expressing broader patterns of relating within the field of non-profit social services. Initially, I saw John and Peter's controversy as a clash of egos trying to change their degree of dependency on the other while I tried to stay neutral. I located the conflict in the individuals and saw John's need to control and Peter's need to rebel as their motives. In contrast to this individual view, Bourdieu claims that locating power within single actors conceals the relational and structural nature of specific power games (2005, p. 205). Therefore, I will start to explore the field.

The organisation arose from parents who were dissatisfied with the public service. John was representing the rebellious spirit and the opposition to the governmental rule-bound bureaucracy. The organisation's trademark was its difference from the public sector services, which was visible through John's continual struggle with public authorities. He resented bureaucratic procedures such as monitoring forms, structures, and authorities and was relentlessly challenging their purpose in relation to the mentally disabled children. Peter disturbed this order when he involved the lawyer. This also related to how they presented themselves. Peter had recently finished a master's degree in management, whereas John proudly presented himself as a self-made manager. Their reactions to formal authorities expressed a tension in the field.

Symbolic capital

According to Bourdieu, it is essential to understand what is valued and important in a specific field to understand power. He termed this 'symbolic capital', which is concerned with positive recognition, esteem, honour, or knowledge (Bourdieu, 2005, p. 195). Symbolic capital is accumulated over time and allows the possessor to wield power and influence in the field (Bourdieu & Wacquant, 1992, p. 98). Bourdieu views politics as a game of power that involves symbolic capital as invisible domination (1977, p. 192). Symbolic capital covers over 'the pursuit of maximum material profit' (ibid, p. 56), which is why the good repute of symbolic capital is easily converted to economic capital (Bourdieu, 1977, p. 195, 1990, p. 119). 'Growth' of the organisation was one example of symbolic capital in the narrative because growth provided prestige, honour, and support. But growth was not discussed openly as financial growth. This was shown when Peter said in our phone conversation that he was sure John wanted to counsel students from the school to the foundation for financial reasons but could not say it in our planning meeting. An accusation about economic capital such as 'you are only in it for the money' would be too strong an accusation and could boomerang on Peter. I was an agent in the field, and I was, too, one who would be honoured and affirmed if I could deliver growth to the organisation. In hindsight, there was pressure on me to facilitate in ways that would secure growth and progress in a harmonious atmosphere.

Symbolic capital and functional collusion in the narrative

In the narrative, we were all subjected to the symbolic capital, which brings honour and prestige in the specific field. In hindsight, I remember several occasions where Peter argued with John but quickly withdrew when John persisted because he could not object without escalating conflicts and risk being accused of disloyalty. I believe Peter had profited from John's ability to create growth in the organisation which had also led to his own continuous promotion. The mail he sent to the boards the night before the board seminar broke this ordinary order. In hindsight, it occurred to me that maybe Peter did not call me after our planning meeting 'just to talk'. He probably called to influence me because I was not just a neutral facilitator but rather an important ally in the political game of power. Peter found a way to disrupt the functional collusion that I described in Project 3, where colluding can be seen as actions that allow conversations to go on without being excluded. Peter was most likely also making alliances with board members, as he had with me, that I just was not aware of. What I had earlier found to be a unique harmonious collaboration within and between the organisations was instead a complex power struggle to gather allies and support where one needs to draw on symbolic capital in the field. Therefore, I will claim that the ability to disrupt functional colluding, as I described in Project 3, without being excluded requires that one draws on the symbolic capital in the specific field.

Bourdieu allows me to see organisational development as political games of power where consultants are manoeuvring in specific fields, constituted by people with symbolic capital. I drew on symbolic capital when I cited authors such as Elias, and I represented authority because they knew I was an experienced consultant, a writer, and a researcher. For consultants to be influential, they need to manage the impression they create and have to understand what is valued in the field in which they operate.

Managing one's impression is, however, not something one can completely control. First, as I argued in Project 2, it is not possible to control how others interpret one's actions and how one reacts to these reactions. Secondly, my actions as a consultant are habitually formed in ways I am not fully aware of. As I argued in Project 3, I can reflexively explore how my thinking is formed, but I can do so only under the constraints of my thinking. So, when we act, we express and represent broader patterns of relating than we are aware of. 'It is because subjects do not, strictly speaking, know what they are doing that what they do has more meaning than they know' (Bourdieu, 1977, p. 79). Bourdieu describes this further with his concept of habitus.

Habitus and the game of politics

Habitus is the internalised external social structure and, in that way, is history turned into nature (Bourdieu, 1977, p. 78). Bourdieu's theory of habitus describes individuals as 'agents with dispositions, preferences and interests that are very different … but adjusted … to the inbuilt constraints of the structure of the field' (2005, p. 216). Individuals reproduce social structures and power differentials because they are embedded in the overall power structures (Bourdieu, 1994, p.

86). Our actions are orchestrated collectively but not produced by a conductor (Bourdieu, 1977, p. 72). Bourdieu's theory suggests a radical decentring of the individual where actions, thoughts, and emotions are habitual responses that express social structures, which means that my incentive to create a harmonious atmosphere, avoid conflict, and be positively affirmed expresses broader patterns of relating. This view is similar to the views on how the individual and the social are related, as expressed by Elias and described in Project 2, and within the perspective of complex responsive processes of relating, as I described in Project 3. This is different from social constructionist approaches to consultancy because the social structures are not viewed as constructions that we can change to the positive by talking or thinking differently about them. We cannot stand outside of the social structure either. We are embedded in the social structure.

We can manoeuvre in the game, though. Bourdieu calls the ability to sense what goes on, and to acknowledge what is at stake, a 'feel for the game' (Bourdieu, 1990, p. 66; Bourdieu & Wacquant, 1992, p. 128). Political action is the art of getting influence which requires a 'feel for the game' and implies a sense of the field, the symbolic capital, and the acknowledgement that everybody else also has a feel for the game and can act upon it. It requires a 'feel for the game' to call out functional colluding, that I described in Project 3 because one needs to understand and have symbolic capital in the field to stay in the game. In this light, one might argue that both Peter and I exercised a 'feel for the game' because we managed to find ways to act and influence the events without being excluded. I engaged in the conversation with Peter between the meetings and challenged John afterwards; Peter allied with a lawyer, and we refrained from disrupting the functional collusion as long as we did not have enough symbolic capital to avoid exclusion. But in my case, I will argue that refraining from acting was not only an exercise of a 'feel for the game'. It also covered over my habitual response to try and make others think positively about me as a consultant who could facilitate events in ways that would lead to growth in a harmonious atmosphere. I was striving to be a neutral helper who avoids negative emotions, rejection, and conflicts, all of which are influenced by broader social patterns of relating as expressed in the literature I referred to within process consulting (Schein, 1987b), dialogic OD (Bushe & Marshak, 2016), and second-order systemic approaches to consultation (Campbell, 1995).

I will argue that Bourdieu's notion of a 'feel for the game' allows for a far more complex understanding of consultancy than the application of generic methods as described in Project 3 (Bushe & Marshak, 2016, p. 408). Bourdieu's notion is not generic in the sense that one has to pay attention to the specific history to understand what goes on in a field. In the narrative, I had to understand how growth and John's positioning of the organisation as 'a movement' in contrast to the public service emerged as a struggle that was represented by Peter and John. I became important as a potential ally for both because I had symbolic capital as an expert on organisational development and as a researcher. I find Bourdieu's concepts valuable for understanding how consultants are participants in political games of power, which involves paying attention to the symbolic capital in the field to understand the expectations towards one's role.

However helpful Bourdieu is, I have reservations about his description of the relation between the individual and 'social structures' (Bourdieu, 1991, p. 235, 2005, pp. 130–131). Bourdieu states that social and economic conditions largely determine an individual's actions (Bourdieu & Wacquant, 1992, p. 136). Bourdieu does acknowledge that the individual has agency but then continues to write that the habitus 'steps in to fill the gaps … to express the socially constituted drives of their habitus' (2005, pp. 130–131). This makes it difficult to describe individual agency and how change emerges. This might follow from Bourdieu's understanding of sociology as he tellingly quotes Bertrand Russell to say that sociology is about how people 'don't have any choice to make' (Bourdieu, 2005, p. 1). His view on habitus as the internalisation of social structures leads to an inadequate theory of individual agency in my view. As an example of my sense of agency, I acknowledge that economic interests, such as promoting the counselling, were important in the narrative. I had economic motives too; after all, I am still working for John. But I am hesitant to assign primacy to economic motives because I did not feel successful just because I was not blamed or because my contract was prolonged. I still felt emotionally affected and constrained, like a puppet on a string, but also that I had a choice and that the choice was about what was right or wrong. Bourdieu was interested in how the subject was objectively formed by social structures and promoted the idea of reflexivity in the sense that we should question how we think, and why we think what we think (Bourdieu & Wacquant, 1992). This has similarities to how I presented reflexivity in Project 2, but Bourdieu's emphasis in his work is on social structures, like class and educational background, whereas my focus is on local interactions between people in organisational work, which draws attention to emotions, thoughts and conversations, and how this might express broader patterns of relating.

Clash between habitual response and 'doing good'

At the board seminar, I experienced a clash between my habitual response as a consultant and a vague notion that 'doing good' would require something other than being a neutral facilitator. I have found Bourdieu helpful in explaining why we acted as we did in the narrative, but I am also interested in exploring what I *should* be doing as a consultant. Bourdieu does not provide an explanation of ethical choices, such as those I faced in the narrative, which is probably because Bourdieu defined his task as a sociologist to describe patterns, not choices. I will explore how I might supplement Bourdieu's perspective to explain what it might mean to act ethically as a consultant.

Doing good as a consultant?

The ongoing inquiry in this thesis has revealed how I earlier interpreted the Christian message of 'love your neighbour' as a universal ethical position to mean that affirming and being nice to others was to 'do good'. I have linked this to appreciative inquiry and the tradition of process consulting which prescribe that affirming others, drawing attention to positive emotions, and avoiding conflict from the position of a neutral helper is to do good. One illustration in the narrative is the attempt to plan the days so they would proceed in a positive atmosphere. In hindsight, I was struggling between the expectations to create a positive atmosphere while, at the same time, recognising a need to address and acknowledge power struggles. My need for a positive atmosphere was also displayed when I sensed a power struggle and offered to use Elias to discuss power relations. This effort was half-hearted in the sense that I eagerly accepted the claim that everyone agreed on the overall values in the movement despite my continued suspicion that this was not so. From a relational perspective on power, I was colluding with the board and John as the most powerful actors, resulting in constraints on speaking up critically for anyone, including myself. One might say that I skilfully avoided open conflict both in planning meetings, the board seminar, and the awayday. But the avoidance of open conflict during the board seminar did not avoid harm. Peter felt he was harmed at the board-seminar. Later on, John was harmed by Peter's mail, followed by sadness when he lost influence over the school. I feared the children were worse off when the organisations were not able to communicate with each other about them. So, doing good cannot be reduced to the role of a neutral helper who creates a positive atmosphere and avoids open conflicts. I have gradually realised that this is closely linked to my own need for affirmation and how I have affirmed others, avoiding negative emotions and conflict to influence others to think positively about me. Lack of positive affirmation arouses bodily reactions in me, and I have argued in Projects 2 and 3 that these reactions are important for understanding what is going on and should not be avoided for the sake of my affirmation.

Due to these reflections, I have shared my reflections and reactions with clients with increasing honesty, as described in this project and in Project 3. This is particularly spurred by my experience with the responses I have received to my work on this thesis from my supervisor, the learning set, and the broader research community on the DMan. I have been preoccupied about whether they were thinking positively about me and my work. I have experienced their responses as extremely critical at times, and it has made me feel disheartened and discouraged. In time, I have found a quality in their responses that is very different from positive affirmation though. In our continued work together, I have learned that their relentless commenting and the time they spend is a genuine effort to improve my work and to help me. I know now that they care for me and that their thorough engagement is crucial to produce robust research that resonates with a broader community, enabling me to draw generalisable conclusions, if only temporarily, about patterns of human relating. This is affirmative in the sense that it is helpful and necessary for me to produce this doctoral dissertation, albeit they are not primarily pointing to positive aspects. Their emphasis has been to comment on aspects that need more work, and their honest responses have allowed me to understand what they think about me and my work. I realise that it is not easy for my colleagues to comment, knowing that it might cause pain, which makes me feel recognised by them all the more. I am curious to explore recognition as an ethical act, and I will explore this from the relational view that has proved relevant to understanding the narratives throughout this thesis.

The French philosopher Paul Ricoeur addresses ethics from this relational view. He is located in the Hegelian tradition and assumes, as Mead and Elias do, 'that the selfhood of oneself implies otherness to such an intimate degree that one cannot be thought of without the other' (Ricoeur, 1992, p. 3). His view on ethics is tied to the interdependency between humans and how one appears to oneself through the other. Authors such as Butler (2005) and Honneth (2003) express similar views on the relation between the self and others, but I have found Ricoeur's philosophy on ethics particularly relevant to explore the puzzle about what it might mean to do good as a consultant in the narrative.

Paul Ricoeur

Ricoeur has written widely about hermeneutics, metaphor, translation, recognition, ethics, and narrative where he draws extensively on Aristotle, Kant, and Hegel. I have found his view on ethics, mutual recognition, and narrative identity relevant to the narrative and my theme of impression management. But it is also difficult to understand where and with whom his thinking starts, so I have sought help from several authors (Joas & Knöbl, 2009; Kemp, 2002; Nussbaum, 2002; Pellauer, 2007; Venema, 2000; Wallace, 2002). My difficulties might illustrate Ricoeur's position as a hermeneutical thinker where 'the meaning of a part can only be understood if it is related to the whole' (Alvesson, M., Skoldberg, 2018, p. 116), which makes interpretations of his work endless (Pellauer, 2007, p. 6). This is similar to my overall approach to research in this thesis, where I have explored how my need for positive affirmation is embedded in broader patterns of relating. I will account further for the methodological implications of this approach in the synopsis.

Ricoeur takes his starting point on ethics with the Latin *mores* as 'that which is *considered to be good* and of that which *imposes itself as obligation*' (Ricoeur, 1992, p. 170 italics in original). He picks up on the philosophical traditions of both Aristotle and Kant and suggests that *ethics* refers to the aim of an action (teleology) and that *morality* refers to the duty to act according to a rule (deontology) (ibid, p. 170). The Christian commandment 'love your neighbour' that I have mentioned as my vague guideline expresses a deontological approach because we are not necessarily drawn to love everyone else, but we should out of duty. I experienced that this was not sufficient to guide me in the narrative because doing good to one would harm others. Nussbaum explains how Ricoeur argues that we still need rules because 'action in society involves power, and the existence of power (of one agent over another, of institutions over agents) always involves the possibility of violence and force' (Nussbaum, 2002, p. 271). But the universality of rules is insufficient to make decisions in the particular situation. Ricoeur argues that ethical choices need to pass through the sieve of the rule, which is a necessary anchor, but not sufficient to decide what to do in the specific situation (Ricoeur, 1992, p. 170). The contextual nature of deciding the good, *ethics*, needs to be enriched by the general view of the right, *morals* (ibid, p. 203). Thereby teleology (aim) and deontology (rule) are connected where the first is primary to the latter.

When I sympathised with Peter but did not manage to speak up, I felt I 'ought' to be doing something else than I did. This is about morals. I ought to be helpful, honest, kind, and supportive. However, that did not help me in the particular situation. Because my support of him might have made his situation worse, excluded myself, and thereby made any further discussion of the issue impossible. In other words, knowing what one ought to do in theory is not a sufficient guide to act in practice. Ricoeur then offers the notion of 'recognition' to guide ethical action in the particular situation. Because it is only through being recognised by others that we understand and thereby recognise ourselves. And others recognise themselves only through our recognition of them. Recognition involves particular people realising themselves through and with the other (Ricoeur, 2005, p. 250). So, to aim for the good life with and for others requires mutual recognition in the particular situation, and it is an ethical obligation to act with solicitude and care towards others, just as they are obliged to act with solicitude and care towards you. Care for the particular other overrules the universal rule (Ricoeur, 1992, p. 190). Ricoeur stresses, however, that mutual recognition is not like an exchange of gifts (2005, p. 219). I will argue that instrumentalised positive affirmation of others, as it is prescribed in appreciative inquiry (Cooperrider, 2013), is not to be confused with recognition. It is quite the opposite; instrumentalised affirmation deprives the other of recognition. This is what I experienced in Project 2 in the conversation that came across as insincere to me because it was in the instrumental form of a feedback sandwich.

An implication of recognition is that we are obliged to make ourselves available and useful to the other (Ricoeur, 1992, p. 268), which I understand as partly giving others access to what we think and feel. In the narrative, I take this to mean that I was responsible for making my convictions available to John and Peter through sharing my reflections with them because I believed they were important for the welfare of the children. But I did not share my reflections and thereby deprived them of the opportunity to engage with what I was puzzled about. They might have acted differently if they had known what I was thinking. The same happened in Project 2 where I was partly insincere when I affirmed Anna and the group. In both instances, I was denying others the possibility to recognise themselves through my recognition of them. Ricoeur's puzzling phrase 'oneself as another' means we are obliged to be reflexively aware of who we are in our relations with others. We are responsible not only for what we do to others but also for who we are through what has happened to us because this has made us who we are: 'Recognising one's own indebtedness with respect to that which has made one what one is, is to hold oneself responsible' (Ricoeur, 1992, p. 295). We can never fully understand or account for ourselves, though. The self will always be, at least partly, 'other' to itself because we do not have full access to how we have been formed by others (Pellauer, 2007, p. 98; Ricoeur, 2005, p. 248; Wallace, 2002, p. 83).

This thesis is an exploration of how I have been formed by others and how this represents broader patterns of relating. I have reflexively explored my need to control the impression I make in others and how this affects my relations. In Project 2, I was trying to control the client's decision and emotions through positive affirmation but found that my need for affirmation controlled me instead. This is also shown in Project 3 with Carl and in the narrative in this project. In that sense, I had less agency when I was dependent on the affirmation of others. This has led me gradually to share more reflections about my thinking with John, but I was not sharing my thoughts as honestly as I was writing about it in this project. I felt an obligation to give both John and Peter access to my reflections. But would it be helpful for them? Would it be harmful? How could I decide whether to share the narrative and my reflections? Since there is no universal rule to guide moral judgements, in specific situations, *phronetic* judgment is required according to Ricoeur (Ricoeur, 2005, p. 88).

Phronesis

Phronesis was originally formulated by Aristotle and can be translated as practical wisdom. 'To direct action, practical wisdom must proceed from universal knowledge to knowledge of the particular' (Ricoeur, 2005, p. 88). In this way, Ricoeur's theory of ethics consists of a triad of aim, rule, and phronesis (Kemp, 2002, p. 40). Bourdieu also refers to phronesis in his expression of 'a feel for the game' where this is seen as the art of maximising symbolic power in the particular field and in the particular situation. I am persuaded by Bourdieu's concepts of field, symbolic capital, and habitus to understand impression management as inherent parts within consultancy as political games. But I have reservations when maximizing symbolic power is viewed as the primary reason for action. I will argue that I was not determined just to maximise symbolic power in the narrative but that it also involved an ethical choice about what to do (Ricoeur, 1992, p. 269). Ricoeur argues that we, as humans, are capable of reflexivity and, therefore, also responsible for the consequences of our actions (Pellauer, 2007, p. 90). According to Nussbaum, Ricoeur means that we are obliged to take responsibility for who we are, the consequences of our actions, and make reparations if necessary (Nussbaum, 2002, p. 273).

I side with Ricoeur when he argues that practical wisdom is about giving priority to decisions that serve the care of particular others in particular situations (Ricoeur, 1992, p. 262). But care does not mean to soothe the other as I have argued. It means to engage and recognise with the other in conversation. 'In this regard, one of the faces of practical wisdom ... is the art of conversation, in which the ethics of argumentation is put to the test in the conflict of convictions' (Ricoeur, 1992, p. 290). Due to the reflections on mutual recognition as an ethical obligation and the exercise of practical wisdom, I felt obliged to share the narrative with John and Peter. I felt it would be unethical not to share my reflections with them. They might be upset, hurt, or angry, but I felt obliged to account for my reflections to them. Earlier, I was terrified that they would not think positively about me, be angry, that John would terminate our work together and perhaps threaten with lawyers if I were to publish the narrative. But I felt that sharing the narrative had become more important than their affirmation of me. Due to my exploration of power, ethics, and recognition so far in this project, I found myself curious and keen to engage in conversation and explore what would happen. I was excited to explore their reactions towards my reflections and ready to face the consequences if they were upset with me. I knew that my habitual approach would be to create an atmosphere of positivity and consensus, so it was clear to me that I needed to be aware of my motives as well as theirs. There was no safe zone from the wish to present oneself in certain ways to others.

Discussing the narrative with John and Peter

With this in mind, I decided to call both John and Peter to explain that I had been writing about them in my thesis and wished to share it with them. They were both willing to read and discuss. Rather than collecting their views, I regarded our meetings as conversations that would create new meaning about our work together with regard to power, ethics, and impression management.

Peter read it quickly and called to schedule a meeting. In our short conversation on the phone, Peter said he could identify with the descriptions in the narrative. He explained how he had felt blindsided by John and had abandoned his ethical principles in the support that he had given to John for too long. I resonated with his experience of a dilemma about speaking up against John, but I also thought that placing responsibility for the events within John's personality was somewhat defensive and self-justifying perhaps out of guilt because we had found ourselves unable to act. I dared to suggest this to Peter because I wanted to act with care by telling him how I felt instead of merely positively affirming him. We conversed for a while. I felt our conversation went in circles where he tried to convince me about John's personality as the primary cause of conflict, which I did not accept. I did not try to find consensus as I would have earlier.

When we met a few weeks later, he said that he had found my argument about their struggles expressing broader patterns of relating helpful for seeing them as broader than personal disagreement between them. He said he had wanted to bring some sort of revenge against John but that, after our discussion on the phone, he did not need to anymore. He also emphasised that our phone conversation about power after the board seminar had been a turning point for him. Viewing the power struggle as a game had given him sufficient detachment to challenge John and had allowed him to come to terms with the events in the aftermath. He felt I had been helpful as a consultant to enable this. I said that I had felt guilty for not acting more in the course of the events to which he replied that he had had no expectations for me to do so. We ended the conversation and agreed to keep in contact.

I met with John shortly after, and I felt more anxious about meeting John than Peter. I traced this to the fact that I still worked for him and that I found John more intimidating in general. I started our conversation by telling him I had felt anxious about this meeting. I added that it had taken me a long time to challenge and speak with honesty about my views in our work together and I had been unsure about whether he would be angry with me about what I had written. John had experienced these reactions toward him before and ascribed it to his passionate views about changing the society. 'The cause', he said, was bigger than himself. It was also bigger than Peter, me, and even the particular mentally disabled children. I questioned whether this was so simple. In my experience, he was quite occupied with what others thought of him, as one that fights for 'the cause' rather than having selfish motives. He agreed. I also asked how he felt about the specific problem about the lawfulness of advising the students to go to the 'foundation'. He said it was merely a way to bring the issue up for discussion. I felt there was more to it, but I did not pursue the issue further. In hindsight, my hesitancy puzzled me, and I will return to this. John continued and said he experienced that my role was to bring my reflections to him and the management group to allow them to reflect on their actions. He said that my presence had allowed him to see how he influenced other people. He had found my reflections helpful for understanding why others often withdrew when he wanted them to engage, explore, and argue with him.

A week later, I met with John and his managers at our monthly meeting. He said he had told them about our conversation. I seized the moment and gave an account of my experience as described above, and it enabled a discussion about how John affects the board, the other managers, and the employees. This led to an exploration about how we all affect each other, and we explored how we can engage with difference and disagreement to a higher degree. The day after, I received an unsolicited mail from one of John's managers who wrote that she was really happy about the meeting, the way their relations were developing, and my contribution to this. This supported my own experience that we were working in a valuable way, which made me happy. Surprisingly, I experienced that I ended up having more of a beneficial impact when I was less preoccupied with impressing them.

Reflections after the conversations with John and Peter

I felt both conversations were valuable for understanding what had happened. But I was also left with the impression that Peter had seemed eager to explain the events as caused by John's personality and that John had presented himself as too altruistically driven. Also, John probably did not want the lawfulness to be an important issue in our conversation because I had already presented it as problematic in the first part of this project which he had read. I wondered in what way they were trying to recruit me to their worldviews and leave a certain impression with me. I did not experience them as manipulative or dishonest in our conversations, but I assumed they were aware that our conversations would be part of this thesis which influenced our conversations.

I was curious or perhaps even suspicious about their motives in the conversations, and I find Ricoeur's expression *hermeneutics of suspicion* useful, as it is presented by Josselson (2004). The hermeneutical approach means that the narrative is to be seen as a part of broader patterns of relating. This means that one needs to be suspicious to allow for alternative interpretations about what is happening and also that understanding ourselves 'is inseparable from an exercise of *suspicion*' (Ricoeur, 1992, p. 341 italics in original). Suspicion is not to be understood as judgmental pejorative doubt but as 'attempts to decode meanings that are disguised' (Josselson, 2004, p. 1). I will use the word 'curiosity' instead because I consider curiosity to be less normatively loaded. This means that I must be curious about my motives, which brings me back to why I did not pursue John further about the issue of lawfulness. I realise that my concern about the continued work relation with John and my need to avoid conflict allowed me to push the conversation only so far. In this light, my task as a consultant might be to insist on being curious and share this curiosity with clients in ways that allow us to move on together.

In sum, I find that the conversations illustrated the point that impression management is always a part of the political games of power in organisational work as well as in research. Conversations are always immersed in power relations, and Peter and John were trying to impress me because I carry the weight of the symbolic capital as a researcher. I realise that consultancy is not just about consultants' need to perform. Consultancy is also about clients managing the impression they make on consultants. Understanding impression management as part of political games of power and the obligation to recognise the other has allowed me to think differently about my experience of the events in the narrative.

Messy consultancy

The experience of a mess started when my position as a helper was challenged. In this narrative, I was recommended to Peter by an old acquaintance. So, who should I help and be loyal to? My acquaintance who, in hindsight, I felt indebted to for the job, Peter who I sympathised with for his rebelliousness, John for whom I still worked and whom I respect for his relentless insistence on helping mentally disabled children, the two chairs who had formally hired me for the seminar and the awayday (they were disagreeing with each other, which made it impossible to satisfy both). Or should it be my sense of what was right or wrong, which continually evolved as we interacted and, as I have argued with Ricoeur, none of us are fully aware of? Peter and John seemed occupied about whether they were good enough in my view but also about how I would present them to others. The latter was particularly the case in my latest conversations with Peter and John, where they knew I was writing about them in this research.

I have argued that consultancy is political with the consultant as a participating political operator. As a self-employed consultant, my reputation is important for being hired in the first place and entails a performance drawing on symbolic capital and performing as an experienced organisational psychologist, author, and researcher. Acknowledging the broader patterns within management consultancy along with Bourdieu's description of power and Ricoeur's ideas about ethics has changed my striving to be positively affirmed. It has allowed me, to a higher degree, to focus on how I act for the good. This led me to send this project at the time where I had written the narrative and the section on power to John and Peter. Although impression management was still a part of our conversations, I experienced that the meetings involved a loss of control over the impression I made on others. I did not feel rejected or that I was rejecting them as I probably would have earlier, and I was less worried about conflict or that they would not think positively about me. I have developed a curiosity towards others' as well as my motives, which I share with clients to a higher degree. But although I had changed, I was still hesitant about challenging John about the lawfulness of his suggestions in our conversation. In that sense, I was still the same because I was worried that he might not think positively about me. This underlines my point from Project 3 that consultants do not stand on the outside of organisations and facilitate or implement changes to others but are participants and are changed by the events too. I will argue the same for Peter and John. Peter was beginning to understand the politics of the situation, which allowed him to act although he still blamed John for the events to some extent in the aftermath. John was beginning to explore how he affects others but still avoided engaging with the lawfulness in the situation. We all changed in some ways and were yet the same in others. Identity and change are at the core of Ricoeur's theory of ethics which I will explore below.

Mutual recognition, narrative identity, and identity change

Ricoeur argues that identity is experienced as a dialectic between sameness and otherness (1992, p. 140, 2005, p. 91). *Sameness* is about character and keeping one's word as the permanence in time in one's sense of self (Ricoeur, 1992, pp. 117–118). 'Character, I would say today, designates the set of lasting dispositions by which a person is recognized' (ibid, p. 121). To be responsible means to account for oneself as the same self over time. We are responsible to be the same so that others can count on us (ibid, p. 165). But we are also, paradoxically, responsible to change at the same time. This relates to *otherness.* Because when we recognise others and take them seriously as individuals, we will inevitably change. In other words, other people interrupt our sense of sameness, which might lead to a loss of identity (ibid, pp. 149–150). Otherness is not only other people however; it is also our own body (ibid, p. 319). By this he means that our body is not our possession. We are thrown into the world that was already there, and we are only gradually 'being delivered over to oneself' (ibid, p. 327). We are obliged to recognise ourselves as another and reflexively investigate what we are subjected to and thereby who we are (Ricoeur, 2005, pp. 91–92). His expression *'oneself as another'* is to be taken literally in this way (Ricoeur, 1992, p. 327). My experience of being a 'puppet on a string' with bodily reactions of being uncomfortable and uneasy is related to Ricoeur's third and last notion of otherness, which is *conscience* or the relation of the self to itself. Ricoeur indicates conscience with the metaphor of 'a call'. He quotes Heidegger: 'The call undoubtedly does not come from someone else who is with me in the world. The call comes *from* me and yet *from beyond me and over me'* (ibid, p. 348 italics in original). We are called upon by ourselves as a voice of conscience, which often takes the shape of guilt, debts or requital; as something unfinished that we need to address (ibid, p. 346). I experienced a 'call' in the narrative in the sense that something was wrong and unfinished for me. As the narrative evolved, I tried to make sense of my bodily reactions and the 'call' of conscience, which I experienced as an ethical obligation to do something different from my habitual response.

Ricoeur thereby argues that individuals are capable of being reflexive about who they are (Ricoeur, 2005, pp. 150–151). Michel (2015) points to an important difference between Bourdieu and Ricoeur here. He argues, as I have earlier, that Bourdieu's understanding of habitus as internalised social structure makes it difficult to explain agency. Michel argues that Bourdieu's habitus and Ricoeur's 'character' both describe the lasting dispositions by which one recognises a person, but that Ricoeur's theory leaves space for a reflexive distance from oneself, which opens up the space for agency (ibid, p. 8). Otherness represents a threat for identity because it interrupts our sense of our 'lasting dispositions or character' (Ricoeur, 1992, pp. 149–150). Otherness feels like a threat because we cannot account for ourselves to others and to ourselves if we are not the same (ibid, pp. 149–150). Ricoeur has coined the 'narrative identity' to describe personal identity as the dialectic between sameness and otherness.

My gesture in the mail I sent after the awayday was an attempt to take a stand about what I thought was right. I reacted on my incentive to do something different, which would hopefully bring them out of their stalemate. But it was also very late in the events, and with little risk involved for all of us. I did not involve a broader audience so Peter and John could both easily get off the hook without appearing uncooperative. For my own part, I had displayed an act of goodwill without getting into conflict, which was, in hindsight, an impression I have been keen to make earlier. I was trying to respond to the 'call' and do something I found important but with a residue in my habitual response as a neutral consultant wanting to avoid potential conflicts. The 'call' has changed me, although I am still the same person. Ricoeur's view on mutual recognition has convinced me to believe that we are obliged to account for ourselves, make ourselves and our convictions available to the other and that we are also obliged to recognise others, which will change us. We must recognise ourselves as otherness but, at the same time, have continuity as a self because this is required to account for and be responsible for our actions. We are paradoxically obliged both to change and stay the same. In this way, organisational change is about change in the clients as well as in the consultant.

Initially, I felt it was wrong of John and Peter to engage in power struggles and that it would be wrong of me to join the struggle. Bourdieu has been helpful for me to realise that it is not only impossible, but also wrong, not to engage in power struggles because they are an inherent part of organisational development. I have experienced a shift in my role from seeing myself as a neutral consultant to see myself as a political operator. This is displayed in my reflections about whether to write this narrative in the first place. In hindsight, I believe my hesitancy originated from the sense of obligation to share my reflections about the narrative, which would conflict with my idea of myself as a neutral helper. Voicing my opinions during the events or sharing the narrative in the aftermath would change my understanding of myself as a consultant. These reflections opened a space to deal with ethics, which required exploring and expressing my convictions. The 'call' gradually allowed me to make riskier gestures as time passed. Making riskier gestures by sending the narrative to participants and sharing my emotions runs through the prior projects and my practice in general. It feels risky because it involves personal change. Ricoeur's idea of narrative identity explains the ongoing self-interpretation in and with others as the movement between sameness and otherness. I will argue that this was also of importance to understand John and Peter's perspectives in the narrative.

Ethics and change

John was the founder of the organisation and his identity was tied to what he had created for mentally disabled children through relentless challenging of customs and authorities. Peter challenged this and John lost not only control over what he had been able to control informally earlier, but also his understanding of someone who had control over decisions that concerned the school; a loss of identity. His immediate reaction was to 'move on' and 'put it behind us', which I regarded as unhelpful for both him and his managers because it closed down further conversation. Instead, we managed to explore feelings of sadness and sorrow. John repeatedly said he appreciated how I challenged what he was saying in our ongoing work, and I experienced these explorations as otherness challenging his selfhood as sameness, which led to new self-interpretations for John. Peter rebelled against John more and more openly throughout the events. I identified strongly with Peter's struggle, and I related it to situations where I had felt intimidated and stayed silent in situations with figures of authority, both in relation to Carl in

Project 3 but also as centre manager in Project 1. I admired Peter's rebelliousness, and I envied his courage to speak up in the power game. But it was an emotionally strenuous process for him. He was disappointing John whom he had to thank for his position and on whom he had been dependent on for affirmation. I believe this was threatening Peter's relation to John and his identity and probably contributed to his resignation. Throughout this thesis, I have been careful to explore curiously how my habitual reaction to positively affirm others and to perform to be positively affirmed might not be helpful to clients. This reflexive engagement has enabled me to take the 'call' in this narrative seriously, stay with the discomfort to reflect on it, which has changed who I am.

Generalising reflections on impression management, power, and ethics in consultancy

It is at those times when I have been unable to control events or manage the impression that I have been making, that emotions have arisen, my identity has been challenged, and I have felt stressed out, lonely, and not good enough. The social and relational character of consultancy has emerged to me in my explorations in this thesis. It has brought my attention to how consultants are social actors, which allows me to ask questions that are, in essence, of an anthropological and sociological research character: What is valued in the organisation and what is the history? I have also been brought to critical and curious questions: Who benefits from my work, and what are my motives?

My work generally felt easier and less emotionally disturbing when I relied on structured planning, personality tests, models, and grids. But, with the benefit of hindsight, I realise that I did not disturb the functional colluding and the existing power relations to the same degree as I do now. Due to this research, I am beginning to ask myself questions about my practice: If I am not going to perform to impress and collude, then what am I going to do? My doctoral studies have stressed how destabilising and terrifying these questions have been for me. My gestures might cause pain but might still be the ethically right thing to do. But it might also be right to collude in other situations. As an example, I could have supported Peter's argument about the law during the board seminar but amplifying his views on the backdrop of the theme of loyalty could have had dire consequences for him. These decisions require the exercise of practical wisdom since interpretations and options to act are without end, according to hermeneutics. Endless interpretations should not restrain us from acting though. Ricoeur elaborates:

> The free access of the pluralism of opinions to public expression is neither an accident nor an illness nor a misfortune; it is the expression of the fact that the public good cannot be decided in a scientific or a dogmatic manner … Political discussion is without conclusion, although it is not without decision (1992, p. 258).

The exercise of moral judgment in specific situations is formed through conversations in public debate and discussions (Ricoeur, 1992, p. 290). I will argue that consultants have a responsibility to find ways to speak up in one way or another about what they believe is right or wrong, debate with others and curiously explore our assumptions with our clients. By sending the narrative to Peter and John, I managed to voice my opinion and talk about something uncomfortable with them with all the risks that doing so entailed. I withstood the uncertainty and my tendency to try to control to be positively affirmed. I acted on my 'call' in my latest conversations with both Peter and John and enabled us to discuss what I found problematic, which allowed us to move forward in the narrative. My incentive to impress the managers in Project 3 and in this narrative was probably also influenced by the fact that I had worked for several years with them. I have noticed how I generally get involved in and am invited to longer-term assignments, and I realise that I am increasingly drawn to a sense of belonging and mutual recognition instead of the immediate positive affirmation involved in winning assignments.

Perhaps consultancy within organisational development is about sharing interpretations, inviting clients to do the same, and exploring the ambiguity that arises. I am not saying that we can circumvent power relations or that inquiries driven by curiosity uncovers truths. But I will argue that consultancy within organisational development is about finding ways to share our curiosity even though this involves the risk of exclusion.

Consultancy as identity change

I argue that the nature of consultancy within organisational development involves continually establishing relations to get and keep jobs and sets the scene for consultants to show themselves to be in control and is particularly ripe for self-blame and stress when lack of control becomes obvious. I have felt pressure on my identity to be positively affirmed. The feeling of failure in Project 1, the rejection in Project 2, the recurrence of disappointment in Project 3, and the 'call' of conscience in this project have all been experienced as threats to my identity. But exploring, rather than denying, the otherness as bodily reactions, other people, and my conscience have allowed me to change in a way where I no longer try to impress with the same intensity. I have changed, but I am still the same. Where does that leave my sense of self? Paradoxically, I feel less fragmented as I have experienced how the mutual recognition that leads to change and loss of selfhood as sameness has also led to belonging. This might be what Hegel described as 'being with oneself in another' (Hegel quoted in Honneth, 2000, p. 29).

I will argue that Ricoeur's narrative identity is useful for understanding the identity pressures faced in working as a consultant. I find that Ricoeur's understanding of sameness and otherness explains how organisational change is also about change in identity for everyone involved. Mutual recognition where one listens to oneself as well as to others is an ethical obligation, which brings about change of identity.

Earlier I have argued that no one can stand on the outside of an organisation. Numerous authors in organisational work (Ericson & Kjellander, 2018; Mallett & Wapshott, 2012; Sparrowe, 2005) argue similarly that Ricoeur's approach accounts for the ongoing development of identity where the self coexists in organisations that are not independent of the self (Ericson & Kjellander, 2018, p. 213). In my practice, I am moving from 'performing to be positively affirmed' to 'being able to go on together', and I am continually exploring, with clients, what it means to be 'good enough' to go on together.

Summing up on the project

I have explored the ideas of Bourdieu and then Ricoeur to explain how consultancy takes place in a specific field with power relations relying on symbolic capital to impress clients. I have concluded that consultancy is inherently political with consultants being political operators rather than neutral facilitators. To understand political games of power within consultancy in processes of organisational development in the narrative, I have drawn on Bourdieu. This led me to see the events as political games of power radically decentring the individual as I explored the field of a non-profit social service provider. Bourdieu's sociological perspective has been helpful to explain how the history within which events take place is crucial to the understanding of events.

I claim that power struggles are an inherent part of consultancy within organisational development that involves a 'feel for the game' which, in short, means to understand and draw on the symbolic capital in the field. The reflections on power led me to understand impression management as an inherent part of these power games. Positively affirming others has been an organising ethical principle of my professional as well as private life played out as being nice to others, staying neutral, keeping a positive atmosphere, and avoiding conflict. But despite the affirmation I received in the narrative as I was continuously hired, I was left dissatisfied, and I gradually found ways to act on this dissatisfaction.

Ricoeur transcends Bourdieu's separation of the social and the individual and advocates an obligation to support care for the other. With this view, I claim that instrumental affirmation of others is the opposite of recognition. Dependency on affirmation can be understood as being lost in oneself, which leads to a position in which one is unable to engage politically and ethically with others. Ricoeur focuses on the individual's responsibility to account for oneself and on the responsibility to recognise other people. He argues further that we are obliged to listen to the 'call' of conscience to exercise practical wisdom. This has been helpful in order to detach myself from my incentive to perform, listen to the 'call' and act upon it. Sending the narrative to Peter and John was my attempt to act with care based on mutual recognition. I have argued that the engagement in organisational development requires care as an ethical obligation that will inevitably change who we are, consultant as well as clients.

My habitual way to perform as a consultant has been to claim neutrality and draw on universal ethic statements and generic tools and techniques. I have found that my efforts to impress others to be affirmed, and the disappointment and shame when this fails, express broader patterns of relating where consultants are under pressure to perform, win jobs, and constantly create relationships. I argue that consultants need to account for themselves and their clients as political agents and exercise practical wisdom, which means expressing their curiosity to disturb functional colluding in politically savvy ways that allow them to move on together with clients. This also means to take an ethical stand with exclusion as a possible scenario. I have argued that we are all responsible for attempting to give an honest account of ourselves and our convictions and that consultants bear the responsibility to insist that those they work with do the same to accommodate an ongoing debate about the ethical judgments we are making, pay attention to the consequences for everyone involved, and make reparations if necessary.

I find myself paying increasing attention to how an ethical practice means taking part in political games of power that involve impression management. I have begun to make riskier gestures to stand up for my convictions and find these to be ethical acts of care. I argue that curiosity as well as giving an account of one's position and convictions are ethical obligations because it allows others to know themselves and, in turn, changes oneself.

Synopsis

In this synopsis, I present my projects, reconsider them reflexively, and develop my research as three key arguments. Lastly, I suggest how my findings might contribute to practice and knowledge within consultancy in organisational development. First, however, I will present the theme of my research as it has emerged, which will lead me to describe my methodology and research ethics.

It is a requirement of the DMan to engage reflexively with one's thinking in the first project and continuously explore the movement in one's thinking as it develops throughout the thesis (Stacey & Griffin, 2005, p. 25). After the first project, I have worked on each of the following projects in this way: I have written the narratives, reflected upon them, discussed them with others, and I have engaged with literature to compare with what other researchers have found on related themes. I have returned to explore the narrative further and have repeated this inquiring process six to nine times. This synopsis represents a process similar to that of each project where new ideas and realisations have surfaced as I have reread the projects. I view the act of rereading the projects in this synopsis within the tradition of hermeneutics, as I explained in Project 4 (Bernstein, 1983, p. 133). In this way, my research theme has been explored in an effort to bring both the local detail from my interactions with others in the narratives and the wider patterns of impressing others into view simultaneously. I find Elias's metaphor of a swimmer and an airman useful to describe how we are involved in everyday life activities as swimmers with little overview. At the same time we are able to obtain some detachment and see our actions in the broader flow of historical change (Elias, 2001, p. 47). A person cannot stand outside their individual involvement and unravel it. Although we are never completely detached, it is still possible to explore the broader patterns of relating through one's local interactions with others. In this thesis, I have explored the need to perform and impress through the local interactions in my practice as a consultant. Rereading the four projects has provided me with opportunities for further detachment. It has led me to explore the academic context further and make distinctions from and explain connections to performance, impression management, individualism, and the economy of consultancy. I have touched upon all of these issues in the four projects, but I will draw more precise distinctions in the course of this synopsis.

Research theme

My iterative approach to research means that my animating question has been developed and refined during the course of the thesis. As I described in Project 1, I joined the DMan with a rather fixed plan to write about competition, and I was puzzled and disappointed when my learning set was not impressed by my plan. Although it dawned on me with reluctance and hesitancy, I realised that my trying to impress them was at the heart of my struggles. I had been sick with stress as a manager, and although I had resigned from my managerial position, I had continued a pattern of trying to impress others by publishing a book, releasing records, and pursuing success as a consultant. The doctoral degree was to be the next scalp on my belt. I imagined how I could re-enter the organisational game in ever-higher managerial positions as if I were in a kind of recovery period. I realised I had been exhausted from my experienced need to perform and impress.

My learning set colleagues resonated with my experience and recognised this in their practice as consultants, although not as strongly as I did. I explored the need to perform to impress further through literature, and I realised that my struggles were generalisable for consultants within organisational development. Gradually I found ways to pay attention to my need to impress rather than merely trying to impress others. This led me to the following research question.

Neither the theme nor the specific methodological approach was planned in detail from the outset. In Project 2, I shared the narrative with the central character Anna to understand her perspective and gain more insight about the other participants. In Projects 3 and 4, I felt an ethical obligation to share my writings with my clients. The curiosity about understanding what we are doing together and the ethical obligation to share my reflections have directed my methodological decisions throughout the thesis. These explorations allowed me to understand better what we were doing together, to help them out of their stuck patterns of relating and to impress them as competent enough to continue to hire me. Due to this research, I find myself sharing my experience about what happens with clients as an integrated part of my practice as a consultant. In this way, my roles as a consultant and as a researcher have turned out to be entangled regarding ethics and method so that being a consultant within organisational development involves exploration and research into people's practice together with them. I will describe how my methodological approach has evolved throughout the process of undertaking this thesis.

Method

My methodological approach takes its starting point from the research tradition in the DMan programme at the University of Hertfordshire (Stacey & Griffin, 2005, p. 10). This theoretical perspective draws on insights from complexity sciences, process sociology (e.g., as Elias described), American pragmatism (primarily influenced by Dewey and Mead), and group analysis (as described by Foulkes) and has been developed as a body of knowledge and practice called the perspective of complex responsive processes of relating (Stacey & Mowles, 2016). I described this perspective in detail in Project 3. As students on the DMan programme, we are obliged to engage, though not necessarily agree, with this perspective and the implications for methodology. I have employed the problem-driven perspective from the pragmatic tradition, where I have carefully considered how to explore the problems and puzzles I have encountered in my practice. This has resulted in a multi-faceted approach to research methodology where I have been inspired by the traditions of hermeneutics and pragmatism as well as anthropology as I have written and reflexively engaged with narratives with an auto-ethnographical approach. I will explain this further below.

Abductive reasoning

From a wider perspective on research, there is often a distinction made between inductive and deductive approaches, whereas abductive reasoning is a less common alternative (Alvesson & Skoldberg, 2018, p. 4). Induction starts with a body of data that allows us to produce explanations that are generalisable. Deduction starts with a theory or hypothesis which we can test and substantiate through data (ibid, p. 5). According to Brinkmann (2012), the American pragmatist Peirce suggested abductive reasoning as an iterative approach (ibid, p. 46). Abduction takes as its starting point experiences that are puzzling—a breakdown in the way we understand the world—and involves inquiry into our theoretical preconceptions to find alternative explanations of our experience (ibid, p. 46). So, instead of building theory from data or testing hypotheses, the researcher keeps trying out arguments throughout the research as he or she engages with both data and theory at the same time.

Research from the abductive perspective involves paying careful attention to breakdowns and mysteries in one's everyday practice (Alvesson & Skoldberg, 2018, p. 387; Alvesson & Kärreman, 2011, p. 97; Asplund, 1972, p. 16). I have paid attention to phenomena that were surprising and incomprehensible as I have been paying attention to my theme of research, and I have tried to stay open 'to following unexpected results and letting these guide further empirical work' (Alvesson & Kärreman, 2011, p. 97). Abductive thinking involves problematising and rethinking dominating theories (ibid, p. 59). This openness to question and contest what I have been taking for granted is an implication of what Bernstein phrases as 'engaged fallibilistic pluralism' (1991, p. 336). I take his phrase to mean that taking a plurality of views into account, through a willingness to listen to others, enables researchers to produce generalisable explanations that are as good as they can get for the moment. This means further that any explanation may be challenged at some point in the future because any generalisable explanation is provisional and potentially fallible. Elias has eloquently described this as 'every later theory develops both as a continuation of earlier theories and yet as a critical departure from them' (1978, p. 182).

In Project 3, I argued that the object of research is not separate from the observer and that no one can observe others from the outside as if they are not a part of what is going on. Stacey and Griffin advocate this view and clarify further that work in organisations can be understood only from 'the local interaction in which global tendencies to act are taken up' (Stacey & Griffin, 2005, p. 9). I have been paying close attention to the local interactions in my everyday work to explore the global tendencies of how impressing others affects organisational development. The anthropologist Tim Ingold draws on the pragmatist Dewey in his view on other people who appear in one's research. '… your relations with others get inside you and make you the being you are. And they get inside the others as well' (2018a, p. 103). Therefore, I have adopted an anthropological position of 'participant observation', and have strived to participate and observe as an embedded but watchful insider while doing research (Czarniawska, 1998, p. 25; Ingold, 2018a, p. 11).

In retrospect, my ability to imagine and reflect on the perspective of others has increased during my research and has enabled me to explore what I am doing together *with* others in my work rather than making studies *of* them in the narratives. This anthropological perspective obliges one to listen to the other (Czarniawska, 1998, p. 21) and 'take others seriously' (Ingold, 2018a). To take others seriously in research means further that 'all who join stand to be transformed' (Ingold, 2018a, p. 25). I regard this as a point similar to Ricoeur's notion of mutual recognition as described in Project 4. I have returned to clients in each project for methodological reasons to explore how others experienced what happened. I also returned for ethical reasons because I felt obliged to recognise clients by sharing my reflections and, in addition, in Project 4, because I felt something was wrong. I returned several times until I had made better sense of it for myself and for my clients. It was challenging and anxiety-provoking to return, and earlier, I would probably have regarded my work as a failure, have felt ashamed, and have fled from it as I wanted to in Project 2. However, it was rewarding to write, reflect with my learning set, read, and return to clients to discuss the narratives and my reflections with them. Returning to clients with potentially conflictual contributions has made greater sense and proved to be less difficult than I feared. This is probably because I find myself less anxious about critique and rejection and more curious and interested in the process of exploring what happens no matter whether this is affirmative of me or not. Mutual recognition of others is thereby not only an ethical obligation but also a methodological consideration in research as well as in the practice of a consultant.

Sharing my reflections with participants in my narratives has been an important way to refine my understanding of impressing others and created an opportunity for my research colleagues to join the production of knowledge. This is paralleled in my practice where I also share my honest convictions and experiences to a larger degree than earlier; I strive to work *with* clients in the spirit of mutual recognition. I will elaborate further on this movement in my practice, but first, I will write about the practice of conducting research on the DMan programme.

DMan research community

Working as part of a community is an important part of my research approach. In the DMan programme, we meet at four-day residentials as a community four times a year, where we follow a structure with lectures from faculty and invited guests, student presentations, discussions of each student's project, and community meetings. Students form smaller groups called learning sets consisting of four students and a supervisor. In the learning set, we continually read, comment on, and discuss each other's projects through several iterations. We have virtual meetings between residentials, and each student has a second supervisor who has read and commented on each of one's projects. The second supervisor reviews the work less frequently and has the important function of reading the work and participating in the learning set with a more detached perspective.

The work is single-authored, and the purpose of the learning set and the wider community is to explore, contest, and express resonance towards the narratives, find patterns in the interactions in the narratives, and discuss our reflections, the literature I draw on, and my arguments. The learning set is both focused on the written work and the dynamics of the group as we interact with each other, whereas the wider community is focusing primarily on the latter. In the residentials, we start every day with a 'community meeting' where all six supervisors and students from each learning set on the programme sit in a circle without an agenda or a facilitator. The purpose of this structure is to explore what happens as themes, reactions, and interactions emerge in conversations. This allows us all to explore and discuss patterns in our interactions that relate to our research. As I have participated in the community meetings, I have experienced a growing awareness about my wish to control the impression I was making on others, and this has allowed me to experiment in my interactions with the group and to explore how others and I react in relation to my incentive to perform to impress. This way of working is inspired by group analysis and critical management scholarship to explore the research theme through the detail of one's interaction with the group and make links to organisational life, as explained by Mowles (2017).

I relate my inquiry in the narratives and my interactions in the research community to literature and theory. This has enabled me to make generalisable claims about performance and impression management in organisational development from the perspective of a consultant. This relates to how I view knowledge. I agree with

Martela as he cites Dewey to argue that 'knowledge' should be regarded as 'warranted assertions' (2015, p. 540). Warranted assertions 'are outcomes of inquiry that are so settled that we are ready to act upon them, yet always remain open to be changed in the future' (ibid, p. 540). Peirce's idea about communities of inquiry, as described by Pardales (2006), Shields (2003), and Martela (2015), is useful to describe how knowledge as warranted assertions is produced in my research. As a community of inquirers, we contest and resonate with the local interactions that I have described in my narratives to make links to similar phenomena more broadly in organisations. Inquiry 'never starts from a neutral *tabula rasa* position, but it takes place through the actions of the inquirer that are shaped by his or her particular world-view' (Martela, 2015, p. 549 italics in original). Knowledge emerges in the back and forth of discussions where we invite comments and revisions from colleagues. The resonance from others may be indicative of the generalisability in our work. In my case, the need to impress was displayed not only in my work with clients but also in the way I have been writing, especially in the first two projects. The way I wrote to impress the learning set was obvious to them but invisible to me as an unconscious habit. Later on, I have been less concerned about impressing the learning set, although my academic work still needs to impress. However, with help from my learning set, I have gained further detachment from my experienced need to impress. The detachment has enabled me to test more ideas and has led to more honest and curious explorations about how it affects others both in relation to my research and in my practice as a consultant.

In sum, we work as an 'experiential group' that offers important material for students 'to reflect on and make links with their everyday practice and become reflexive about it' (Mowles, 2017, p. 11). The reactions and reflections that arise as we work in the group have been vital 'data' in order to understand my theme of research. I regard data, from Brinkmann (2014, p. 724), to encompass everything that is related to my theme of performance and impression management: the narratives, my emotional reactions as well as the reflexive process of inquiring into them with both learning set, the wider DMan community, and clients.

The assumption of interdependency with others is fundamental in the work of a community of inquirers. This has been difficult for me to acknowledge in more than one sense. First, it challenged my fundamental expectation that I should perform and impress by producing work in solitude as an autonomous individual. I have written the words in this thesis, but they contain the curious and critical voices of others without whom I could not have produced this work as it was produced in response to those voices. Second, and more generally, I used to relate strength and success with independent individual performance whilst I have viewed dependency on others as a weakness. I explore this as a broader pattern of individualism in the key arguments because it relates to consultancy more generally. In relation to the process of research, I tried to impress the learning set, and it was difficult for me to receive their comments and reflections, particularly at the beginning of this programme. The learning set has been vital as they have shared their reactions and reflections and have invited and even insisted on my engagement with their comments. I have been surprised, disappointed, disheartened, defensive, ignorant, and hurt, as I have received their comments in writing and in conversations. I have learned that this is a common pattern for students. I have gradually realised that their views as well as my reactions are generalisable in terms of my research theme and that collaborative work with a community of inquirers, such as the learning set, means that it is necessary to take the detail of the interaction with others seriously. In general, I relate the disturbance I have experienced to Dewey's approach to reflective thinking. 'Reflective thinking … involves willingness to endure a condition of mental unrest and disturbance. Reflective thinking, in short, means judgment suspended during further inquiry; and suspense is likely to be somewhat painful' (1910, p. 12). This brings me to the reflexive nature of this research.

Reflexivity

In project 3, I described how reflexivity means to take one's way of thinking into account and how this cannot be separated from one's emotional reactions. One should approach breakdowns, mental unrest, perplexity, hesitation, and doubt with curiosity (ibid, p. 9). As Dewey puts it, 'The wisest of the Greeks used to say that wonder is the mother of all science … The curious mind is constantly alert and exploring, seeking material for thought, as a vigorous and healthy body is on the qui vive for nutriment' (ibid, p. 22). As I argued in Project 4, curiosity should be directed to one's own, as well as to others', assumptions. According to Bernstein, both those writing in the traditions of pragmatism and hermeneutics advocate the perspectives that we cannot take complete doubt, the Cartesian position, as our starting point because there 'is no knowledge without *pre*conceptions and *pre*judices. The task is not to remove all such preconceptions, but to test them critically in the course of inquiry' (Bernstein, 1983, p. 128 italics in original). For example, from my second project, I found myself affirming the clients, but I was not positively affirmed by them in return, which made me try harder to impress them. In my reflexive inquiry into the narrative, I realised how I was trying to control their decision-making through positive affirmation but that my yearning for positive affirmation controlled my actions instead. My experience of a breakdown, as I described it with Alvesson and Skoldberg (2018, p. 387), and the inquiry into my assumptions with my learning set combined with literature studies revealed how I performed to impress the clients so they would think positively about me.

I have brought the pragmatic research tradition into conjunction with the hermeneutic approach I employed in Project 4. Hermeneutics and pragmatism are often regarded as supplementary to each other methodologically (Bernstein, 1983; Brinkmann, 2012; Sandberg & Tsoukas, 2011, p. 341). Both hermeneutics and pragmatism are founded in the Hegelian tradition and thereby both view knowledge as fallible and, respectively, as hermeneutical interpretations (Cunliffe, Luhman, & Boje, 2004, p. 275) or as warranted assertions (Martela, 2015). Hermeneutics, in its particular focus on interpretation of text and language (Bernstein, 1983, p. 126), draws attention to 'the relation between the interpreter and what he or she seeks to understand' (Bernstein, 1983, p. 137). Cunliffe draws on Ricoeur to regard research in itself as a narrative (Cunliffe et al., 2004, p. 272). Research relies on interpretations, and it is an ethical responsibility for the researcher to give an account of their interpretations and position of power (ibid,

p. 262). The researcher is part of the research, so to speak. 'A character is the one who performs the action in the narrative... characters, we will say, are themselves plots' (Ricoeur, 1992, p. 143). The significance of this quote is that although the thesis consists of reflexive narratives, it is also a narrative in itself, and that part of the plot in the thesis is the description of my movement as a character.

Narratives and auto-ethnography

I have described and inquired into my practice through written narratives from my practice with an auto-ethnographical approach. I have selected the specific narratives because they have presented a breakdown in relation to my theme. I have tried to convey the events as detailed accounts of what happened at a particular time and place, which 'entails an account of the intentions, expectations, circumstances, settings, and purposes that give actions their meanings' (Greenblatt, 1997, p. 16). Narratives are well-suited for giving a rich account that allows for a systematic reflection about the practice in question because they force one to write about entanglements and how they change over time (Czarniawska, 1998, pp. 76–77). I have been inspired by the discipline of anthropology as *philosophy with the people in* (Ingold, 2018a, p. 4 italics in original) to understand taken-for-granted assumptions, and I have employed auto-ethnography as a methodology. Ethnography is an open exploration into a social world to describe a culture in order to understand how others perceive the world (Spradley, 1979, p. 3). It was pioneered by anthropologists to describe foreign cultures but has developed to include one's own society as well (Ingold, 2018a, p. 121). Ethnography 'does not represent a coherent and clearly prescribed methodology; rather, it indicates a general research orientation, which can then assume a variety of forms' (Alvesson & Skoldberg, 2018, p. 107). Auto-ethnography involves being particularly reflexive about one's impact on the social world that is being described and seeing the research as a social process between self and other (Ellis, 2007). Auto-ethnography means to describe ('graphy') the researcher's personal experiences ('auto') to examine the broader context of that experience ('ethno') (Brinkmann, 2012, p. 79).

Auto-ethnography as an approach for the study of work in organisations has the advantage that I do not have to set up artificial additional meetings because I am studying my own and others' everyday practices (Alvesson, 2009, p. 159). Also, interviewing or observing people as the only way to explore the theme would display our incentive to impress in that particular situation, as I described in Project 4. I have found the broad auto-ethnographic approach appropriate to study how the experienced need to impress others affects organisational development. However, auto-ethnography also includes challenges and limitations. Since the starting point of the analysis is with my personal experience, the research might also be 'limited in its conclusions' (Méndez, 2013, p. 282). Further, it requires honesty, willingness, and the ability to self-disclose (ibid, p. 282). To address these challenges, I have explicitly worked in collaboration with others to find resonance, to discuss the ethics of the research, and to point to my blind spots. Being reflexive about one's practice requires collaboration, as it is found in the ideas of the community of inquiry that I described earlier.

Delamont (2007) claims that auto-ethnographies are mere descriptions of personal experience leading to a lack of analytic outcome. I find this criticism relevant if research relies solely on personal accounts. I am arguing that to claim generalisability requires more than descriptions of one's own experience. This has to be explored reflexively in a community of inquirers and contested with theory in order to explore the broader context of the experience. This is inspired by Anderson's approach to auto-ethnography as analytic rather than evocative (2006) and involves that the researcher is '(1) a full member in the research group or setting, (2) visible as such a member in published texts, and (3) committed to developing theoretical understandings of broader social phenomena' (ibid, p. 373). I have argued, from a Hegelian position, that the latter is possible since the individual is radically social, and that thinking does not start from nowhere. Rather, we inherit categories of thought (Mowles, 2015, p. 30). Therefore, we can explore the broader context of our individual experience with a community of inquirers.

This gives rise to a tension between my critique of individualism in Project 2, which I substantiate further in Key Argument 1, and my methodological approach which might be seen as assigning primacy to my individual experience as the starting point of my research. I acknowledge how the self is a 'modern invention' and that 'the use of the first-person pronoun reflects a specific linguistic tradition, emergent in some (but not all) cultures and languages in which the concept of the individual is lent primacy over that of the collective' (Vine et al., 2018, p. 7). However, I am writing about my practice of working with others which is not just an individual experience. Making an impression implies others from the outset and the method I have adopted is putting the social back in the self, so to speak. I have carefully paid attention to relations, the patterns of interaction, the complexity, paradox and messiness associated with the world of consultancy and organisational life more generally. So, although this work takes its starting point with me and the other individuals that appear in this thesis, paradoxically it is *not* about me or any of the individuals.

Another challenge I have experienced has been that of giving a detailed account of what happened and paying attention to the reactions of others in the narratives, particularly in situations where I experienced strong emotions myself. That was why I returned to Anna in Project 2. I agree with Alvesson and Sköldberg as they view conversations as explorations about how I and others continuously make sense of events (2018, p. 369). I have regarded those to whom I returned to have conversations as fellow mystery detectors (Alvesson & Kärreman, 2011, p.105). In Projects 3 and 4, I returned and shared the narratives with the clients to explore how we made sense of the events and to reflect further together but also because I felt indebted to the clients. Feeling indebted to clients is usual, according to Gosovic (2019, p. 68), as relationships develop while doing ethnography. I did not regard their views as truths about what had happened, though, and I became aware of how my clients were trying to impress me in the conversations in Project

4. Another challenge related to auto-ethnography has been that the managers in Projects 3 and 4 were aware that I was doing research. Although I have been hired specifically to conduct consultancy tasks, several clients have told me it has been interesting and attractive for them to work with me because I was also a researcher. This has affected our interactions, and it is important to explore reflexively how that has affected our interactions, as I did in Project 4.

Ellis has described auto-ethnography as a 'back-and-forth movement between experiencing and examining a vulnerable self and observing and revealing the broader context of that experience' (2007, p. 14). I resonate with the vulnerability of losing control of the image I was trying to project of myself. This was related to identity but also to the politics of my work where the ability to present oneself as competent influences whether one gets and keep tasks in the future (Alvesson, 2009, p. 166). I have tried to follow Gosovic's prescription: 'Rather than subscribing to an illusion of independent research … we as organizational ethnographers get entangled with the fields that we study' and should explore the 'implications this might have for our practices and representations of these fields' (2019, p. 66). All the above is played out in the interactions in the thesis, and I have tried to describe and explore the entanglement, rather than avoid it, to understand the theme of impressing others within consultancy.

To understand the perspective of others in the narratives, I have also drawn on Larsen and Friis's work on improvising in research and carried out a series of role plays with other doctoral students where we replayed events to understand how others might have been affected in the situation (Larsen & Friis, 2017, p. 350). For example, I acted as myself and my research colleagues played the roles of Anna and her colleagues in the events in Project 2. This allowed us to explore and reflect upon how others in the narrative might have experienced what happened and led me to contact Anna again to explore the events with her. Despite my efforts to understand the perspective of others, I am well aware that the narratives are descriptions from my perspective and, although I staged role-plays and had discussions with many of the participants from the narratives, I do not have any direct access to how they might have experienced what happened. Their accounts are, as I argued in Project 4, always conveyed from a particular position influenced by their intentions and our power relations and must be viewed in the context of politics and ideology (Alvesson & Kärreman, 2011, p. 111). John and Peter seemed conscious about the impression they were making, which I ascribed to their knowledge about my depiction of them in this research. In other words, their incentive to impress aroused my suspicion towards their motives. I have encountered this suspicion with curiosity and reflexivity, and I have turned to literature to gain detachment from the particular practice I am embedded in (Alvesson & Skoldberg, 2018, p. 333). My research is interdisciplinary and draws on literature and a range of theories that have emerged out of the disciplines of philosophy, psychology, anthropology, and sociology. I have chosen literature and theories that have been helpful in understanding what we have been influenced by in the narratives. Readings across disciplines have been necessary to understand my theme, develop arguments, and draw generalisable conclusions. With an interdisciplinary approach to theory, and a multi-faceted methodological approach, it is important to avoid shallow eclecticism (Alvesson & Skoldberg, 2018, p. 333). I have approached this challenge by aiming for a thorough argumentation about the relevance of the methods and theories that are drawn in with regard to the specific narrative.

Each narrative has been rewritten numerous times due to the reflexive engagement where themes and reactions that were unnoticed or underdeveloped in the prior iteration have been described further. I have not changed my descriptions in the narratives about what happened as such, but I have elaborated on details. The explicit reflexive engagement with the narrative in a community of inquirers and the commitment to search for the most plausible account of reality rather than inventing situations separates it from a fictional account (Stacey & Griffin, 2005, p. 23). In sum, the reflexive engagement with narratives involves writing, discussing with one's learning set and clients, and wide reading. The auto-ethnographical approach to describe personal experiences in narratives allows me to make generalisable 'warranted assertions' about how consultants' experienced need to impress affects the practice of organisational development.

This thesis, and research in general, is also a performance undertaken to impress others in ways that are recognised in academia. Performing to impress is inherent in research where the thesis must be persuasive within certain rules and norms that are historically formed—understood as the social object, as I described in Project 3 (Mead, 1925, pp. 265–266)—as part of academic traditions. This is not the full picture, though, because although a work of scholarship needs to impress, it is also a product of hard and thoughtful labour with the aim of producing warranted assertions that contribute to knowledge, and my research involves other people towards whom I have a responsibility. This is similar to Project 4 where I claimed that impression management is inherently a part of the political game, although consultancy is certainly not only about persuasion and impression management. It is also about ethics and identity. This brings me to the ethics involved in my research.

Research ethics

I have taken seriously the underlying principle in the ethical approval form to do no harm as a researcher. Doing no harm is a guiding principle in my work as a consultant too. It is a moral rule, but, as I argued with Ricoeur earlier, moral rules are not sufficient to guide decisions in practice. This is viewed similarly by Ellis with regard to auto-ethnography: '... there are no definitive rules or universal principles that can tell you precisely what to do in every situation or relationship you may encounter, other than the vague and generic "do no harm"' (2007, p. 5). In Project 3, the managers could have expressed a preference that I should not use the narrative, which would have denied others access to a narrative that might be valuable to read and learn from. So, what might be harmful to some might be helpful to others. In Project 4, my descriptions might have hurt John initially but could turn out to be helpful later on in the same way that comments from my learning set were often painful at first but have become helpful for me. Ultimately, we do not know how our actions will influence others, and this can change over time. This is relevant in my research but also in my work as a consultant since the nature of both is to engage with others without knowing how it will affect them at the time and in the future. I will argue that the approach to ethics in consultancy I described in Project 4 is equally relevant as a researcher here. Both auto-ethnography and consultancy require practitioners to make ethical decisions in the particular situation. Thus, I have made ethical decisions that have passed through the sieve of the moral rule to do no harm in the projects.

I have informed those I have worked with that I have been conducting research that involves writing about my practice, and I have informed them that I will anonymise the people in my research. However, the participants in Projects 3 and 4 knew I was doing this research and would probably recognise each other and themselves in my descriptions. They might disagree with my recollection of events and how I have described them and their motives. Even if they would find my presentation to be fair, they might feel that I was disclosing confidential material or that I was describing intimate details about their intentions that they would rather have kept secret from others (Armstrong-Gibbs, 2019, p. 240). In my view on mutual recognition, I have advocated for an obligation to take others seriously, which applies to both research and the practice of organisational development. I have argued that consultants as well as researchers are obliged to strive towards sharing their reflections as an ethical responsibility to care for those involved in our research (Ingold, 2018b, p. 49). Care means to listen carefully to those who appear in my research and to take them seriously (Ingold, 2018a, p. 27). I have felt this way in relation to all the people in the narratives. Anna, John, Peter, Carl, their management teams, but also towards my learning set, supervisors, and my parents.

I agree with Ingold as he argues that research is about 'mutual indebtedness. As such, it entails both curiosity and care… We are curious *because* we care … curiosity and care are two sides of the same coin' (2018b, p. 71 italics in original). Taking others seriously has had ethical as well as methodological implications, as I mentioned earlier. The iterative nature of abductive thinking and the unpredictable direction of the research make it impossible to ask for detailed consent in advance. I argue that ethical considerations must be made throughout the research. Therefore, I have sent Projects 3 and 4 to the participants and asked whether they need further anonymisation which they have found unnecessary. These returning conversations have led to valuable discussions with the clients about our work together and have strengthened my belief in the value of continually sharing reflections with clients in my practice as a consultant. Taking others seriously has developed and intertwined as method, research ethics, and a consultancy practice.

In the following, I will briefly summarise the four projects and reflect on this movement in my practice as a consultant.

Project 1: An exploration of recognition and values

In the first project, I described how I have become who I am in relation to others and how this influences my work in organisational development. This is described as an experiential autobiography by Mowles (2017, p. 228). In Project 1, I explored how I was brought up in a family with Christian values and a belief in hard work. I discovered how I have struggled to adapt and excel in schools, sports, work, music, and more throughout my life. I studied psychology, and in my work in organisations, I found that tools and techniques—such as strategic plans, personality profiles, models, and grids—signified that, although problems can be complex, it is possible to create desired results. Appreciative Inquiry (Cooperrider, 2013) stood out as particularly influential for me as it resonated with my understanding of Christian values as a way to do good to others, secure a positive atmosphere, and it appealed to me as a way to be positively affirmed.

When I was a manager in the field of social work, I was continuously promoted. I was proud of my accomplishments and felt I stood out as an extraordinary individual. Eventually, I experienced a breakdown due to a crisis that emerged while I was a manager of a centre where parents of a disabled child secretly recorded the staff and published the recordings. National media were involved, and the politicians and senior management in the municipality reacted strongly. I found myself in a situation I could not solve and struggled with sleeplessness, chest pains, headaches, and nosebleeds for more than half a year. I felt a loss of control, that I was unfairly treated, and I resigned. I was ashamed that I had not been able to solve the situation.

After this, I went back to work as a self-employed consultant, and I started on the DMan to make sense of what happened and to find sophisticated ways to understand and solve complex situations, like the one I had found unsolvable. I made plans about how to manage this thesis and finish ahead of schedule with profoundly original research. However, my learning set relentlessly drew attention to my need to impress them, so instead of trying to control my research, my reflexive work in Project 1 led me to explore how and why I try to control how others think about me, always in a positive light where possible. I acknowledged that everyone likes the idea of others thinking well of them, but I realised how I was taking it further than most, and I became determined to explore how this affects what I do as a consultant and how this might resonate more broadly in organisational development.

Reflexive turn

Rereading the first project highlights how important others' evaluation of me was at the time. The way I described my problems in the children's home in Project 1 was a very singular account and an extraordinary breakdown, but it revealed my need for recognition beyond the particular situation. It pointed to a strong need to stand out as an independent individual where the outcomes relied on my individual achievements. However, my expectations of what I could control and achieve as an individual were inflated. Suffering the consequences of this limited control and agency caused the strong emotional reactions, such as disappointment, embarrassment, and shame. In Project 1, I initially blamed the upper management for being irresponsible and concerned only about covering their backs. I thought resigning was a responsible act in the situation, though now I think differently about my responsibility in the situation. I did not voice my experience of injustice as a manager in Project 1, primarily because I was afraid that others might not think positively about me. In hindsight, I felt successful as an independent individual when I was positively affirmed by others. Obviously, it is a contradiction to be dependent on others to be independent, and I have realised that I am dependent on others for more than positive affirmation. I am dependent on help, challenges, disagreement, grievance, conflict, and much more, and I have gradually realised that others are dependent on me to do the same. In short, we are all engaged in mutual recognition as Ricoeur has described it (1992, p. 193).

The senior management in Project 1 might have acted differently if I had voiced my convictions. To be fair to them, I did not give them a chance to understand my perspective because I did not raise my voice. They might have been more dependent on me than I realised at the time, and I could probably have had more influence if I had viewed us as interdependent, as Elias suggests (1978, p. 78). Bourdieu's understanding of political games of power would have allowed me to take account of the symbolic capital of the situation to gain influence and, with a feel for the game, stay in it (Bourdieu & Wacquant, 1992, p. 128). In hindsight, I regard the incidents I described in Project 1 as a 'call' of consciousness that took the shape of guilt, debt, or something unfinished, as Ricoeur has described (1992, p. 346). I realise now that I felt—and still feel—guilty for betraying the children because I did not speak up and withdrew from the conflict. In my exploration of ethics in Project 4, I argue that it is an obligation for consultants to voice their convictions as a response to the call of consciousness at the risk of conflict and exclusion. At the time of writing Project 1 I experienced that my manager's advice to withdraw from giving support and help to the institution was 'unethical'. I experienced the situation as a breakdown because I felt my values were conflicting, and I couldn't find a response to the situation. As I reflect on the experience now, I find Ricoeur helpful to understand the experience as a 'call' of consciousness. A call to explore further what was important in the situation and how this involved ethics, politics and identity as I described in Project 4. Ricoeur's ideas about mutual recognition do not provide a universal code of ethics or simple answers to apply in the situation. Invoking Ricoeur's ideas are to be seen in the spirit of problem-driven research where the aim is to find explanations that can understand the problems and breakdowns in the particular situation. The metaphor of a 'call' was helpful to understand the diffuse and uncomfortable experience of something that was 'unethical' in Project 1.

I will briefly clarify that I regard the notion of convictions as similar to the notion of values, which I used as a term in Project 1. I regard both from a pragmatic perspective (Stoltz, 2020, p. 65) and not as values or convictions that one can have, but values that one is committed to. '... values are not something we have, or own; it is rather that values own us' (2020, p. 65). I am not saying that consultants always know the values they are committed to, but I am suggesting that they engage in the exploration of them, particularly in the face of a 'call' of conscience. I believe this insight would have made me act differently as a manager in Project 1.

In Project 1, I explored how my striving to adapt, excel, and stand out as an extraordinarily skilled individual solving situations in solitude also led to feelings of isolation and loneliness. Through the persistent exploration with the learning set I have come to know that being positively affirmed has been, and still is to some degree, particularly important to me. Rereading the project accentuates how I felt it was me against the world at the time. In a way, it was a stereotype of the lonely hero. However, I began to acknowledge how I was dependent on the learning set as a community of inquirers to explore my practice and my narratives. I have realised how it is difficult for me to acknowledge my dependency on the learning set because I had associated dependency with weakness.

These experiences of weakness, disappointment and a need to perform to impress as competent are influenced by my specific background as described in Project 1. My specific background relates to demographics of being a male, Scandinavian, influenced by Christianity and a Protestant work ethic and as a formally trained psychologist. Others who share these demographics might resonate immediately. However, the aim of a doctoral studies is to contribute to knowledge and to the practice of organisational change beyond these specific demographics. This is accommodated through reflexive work that involves paying attention to the experience of the breakdown. The breakdowns are explored reflexively in a community of inquirers and contested with theories that are helpful in order to explore the broader context of the experience with the aim of making a contribution to knowledge and to the practice of organisational change. I will stress the importance of keeping in mind how these demographics impact on this research. I have paid attention to how the self in my accounts involves my specific sense of self and the construction of self as a 'modern invention' (Vine, Clark, Richards, & Weir, 2018, p. 7). Therefore, I have described my specific background in Project 1 to acknowledge how one's life history has a bearing on how one think. In the subsequent projects I explore whether and how this is relevant to others (i.e., people from different countries, male/female etc). I will describe further how this allow and constrain me from generalising my descriptions within organisational life in the contribution-section later in this synopsis.

At the end of Project 1, I was particularly interested in exploring what I had encountered as an unconscious need for others to think positively about me as a consultant. The reflexive inquiry has made me pay attention to this as a generalisable pattern about the experience of a need to perform and impress as an individual. I was beginning to think that the thoughtless pursuit for positive affirmation was problematic because it affected the ability to pay attention to relations, interdependency, power, and ethics in processes of organisational development. This exploration continued in Project 2.

Project 2: Control, affirmation, and emotions

In Project 2, I explored a situation where I was rejected for a job, which aroused strong emotions. I was contacted by Anna about a job where I would meet monthly and reflect with her and her colleagues about their job challenges. She said I had been recommended, and although I initially declined because of a busy calendar, I was talked into meeting with her and her colleagues about the job. Because I had been recommended, I had expected a supportive atmosphere but found out that they were not all in favour of my suggestion of working with less structure. I responded to this opposition with a competitive approach, and I suddenly found myself trying to convince them to work with me. Later, Anna told me that they had decided to hire another consultant. I was disappointed and ashamed, and I tried to hide these feelings from Anna and myself. The moment after, she encouraged me to apply for a job as their manager, and I felt happy and proud. This was an emotional rollercoaster, and I did not experience events as if I were controlling them but rather that they were controlling me.

In my reflections on the narrative with the learning set, I realised that working with less planning felt like a loss of control that aroused feelings of anxiety and incompetence in me as well as in the group. During the meeting, a majority of the group members were negative but did not speak up, and I noticed that Anna and I said nice things to soothe each other both before, during, and after the meeting. I found that this made it difficult for us to explore negative feelings and critical comments. I experienced that positive affirmation functioned as an evaluation of my performance and that their rejection was disturbing because it challenged my identity as someone who can get positive affirmation and win in a competition if I put effort into it. I experienced a diffuse loss of control. This loss of control involved emotions, and I wanted to explore how it might be linked to identity.

In my exploration of identity, I draw on the sociologist Norbert Elias whose contribution can be described as process sociology. He rejects a crude choice between looking at either the individual or the social when explaining social change (Elias, 1978, pp. 146–147). He is interested in the interdependency between individuals and how our understanding of identity is embedded in historical processes. Elias describes how the quest for meaning is historically located in the individual, which creates a need to stand out as an individual (1986, p. 53). To make sense of my emotional reactions from this perspective, I draw on Wetherell (2012) and Burkitt (1999), who build on Elias's process sociology and view emotions as relational expressions in a specific historically located practice. This means that my experiences of disappointment and shame were not just 'inner' feelings, but expressions constituted by our social relations. The exploration of disappointment and shame as specific unwanted emotions are, therefore, important parts of learning processes, but they are often suppressed as negative emotions that threaten our identity. I discovered that when I was curious about what happened *with* Anna and the group, instead of evaluating events in terms of success or failure, I was able to explore what had unfolded between us as a group with curiosity. The reflexive engagement with the narrative allowed me to conclude that the exploration of disappointment involved important learning.

Reflexive turn

The change in my view on competition and positive affirmation in my practice is evident as I reread the project, and I will describe a short narrative that describes a recent course of events that displays differences in my practice compared to the events as they played out in Project 2.

In 2018 I had been hired to meet monthly with a group of internal consultants in a public health department. I was contracted by their manager, and we had agreed to work with the group to explore the following questions: 'What were they doing together in their work, why were they doing it, and how did that affect them?' The manager of the team resigned shortly after I had started to work with the group, but we agreed to continue my work with them. A new manager started after three months, and I suggested that we met. She did not have time then but returned six months later and needed to meet with me. She had heard that we had been discussing the new quality standards that the politicians had decided due to budget cuts, and she was worried that my conversations with the staff could support or even create an atmosphere of disloyalty against the standards. I understood her concern and explained we had been exploring how they were making sense of the quality standards in relation to their work. I had, in my opinion, been loyal to both the group's needs and to the organisation's quality standards. I noticed with myself that I started to feel a bit annoyed with the manager because she had not accepted my invitation to have this discussion earlier. I was also irritated with myself for not insisting on meeting with her earlier on. I was paying close attention to my emotions during the meeting, and I regarded them as data or information to understand what was important in the situation. I realised how finding ways to make sense of budget cuts with staff can be extremely sensitive and that she was probably struggling to balance her support for the staff while still appearing loyal to the political decisions. She probably found that I was disturbing this process and possibly perceived me as a threat to her position as a manager. I tried to explain my views, but I felt our conversation was running in circles and that I was not helpful to the organisation because of my relation to her. She clearly wanted to terminate my work with the group. I tried to put myself in her position and imagined she could be concerned that I would critique her on my way out. I was not interested in that though, so I suggested that I should meet one last time with the group to evaluate our work together, which we agreed on. In my last meeting with the group, we all expressed how we were sad that our work had to finish, but we also managed to explore and evaluate how our work together had been helpful for them instead of locating blame with the manager or me for stopping our work.

I have chosen to present this short narrative to highlight the movement in my practice and the contribution of the theories I have drawn on in this thesis. Reading Elias (1978) has enabled me to see consultancy as a political activity that involves power as dependencies. Bourdieu (2005) has been helpful for understanding the new manager's need to be in charge as symbolic capital in this specific situation. Consultants need to understand the symbolic capital in the specific field and have a feel for the game to stay in it. In this case, though, as events developed, I did not stay in the game. Ricoeur's thinking about the obligation to stand up for my convictions as mutual recognition (1992, p. 268) led me to make decisions that terminated the work with the client. I believe I understood the game in the narrative but held on to my convictions about how to work as a consultant. This was possible only because I had gained some detachment from my imperative to impress others. In contrast to my experience in Project 2, I did not yearn for affirmation from the manager or the group to the same degree as earlier, and I did not experience a rollercoaster of emotions as I was facing her rejection. I was able to take a more detached perspective to pay attention to the specific power relations, as well as my need to impress and to be affirmed. I managed to endure that the manager was not happy about my contribution and did not affirm me positively. I also acknowledged that it was not possible—not even my responsibility—to create a harmonious atmosphere between myself and the manager. However, I felt responsible to make an effort so that the manager and the group could continue their work together.

Performing to impress was my default response to the complexity of the situation in Project 2, and when I did not get the job, I was emotionally distressed and lost in my need for affirmation. My preferred reactions in both Project 1 and 2 was to avoid dealing with those harmful feelings. I also realise how my incentive to perform might lead to self-perpetuating spirals, as seen in Project 2, where I tried to present myself as ever more competent instead of engaging in the difficulties that arose in our meeting. I was not paying attention to how Anna was trying to ally with me to change the dynamics of the group and how Anna was dependent on me to change the power relations in the group. I did not pay attention to these relational interdependencies and the politics of the situation because I was tied up by my emotional reactions and my need for affirmation. When she did affirm me, I became suspicious of her motives. I have realised how performances that seem staged to impress, as when people try hard to impress, often cause suspicion towards the motives of others. As I tried to ally with Anna and persuade them to work with less structure and plans, I was not thinking about the consequences in terms of what these changes would mean for the group and how they could find a way together. I hope I have developed sufficient detachment from my need to impress since then, as well as a greater reflexive capacity to approach the complexity in similar situations with curiosity rather than with a pre-eminent need to be positively affirmed. Inspired by Ricoeur's thinking, I feel obliged to pay attention to my need to impress and, in that way, hold myself responsible for my actions (1992, p. 295). I have argued further, assisted by Ricoeur, that responsibility also means standing up for my convictions and facing the possible consequences. This might lead to a clash of interests and conflicts that might terminate contracts, as it did in the short narrative in this reflexive turn. Looking back on Project 2, however, I believe that there was not a gulf of difference that would have prevented me from working with the group. In Project 2 I wrote that the way Anna and I were affirming each other to serve our individual interests and to avoid engaging in negative emotions were dishonest and thereby ethically problematic. In hindsight, I had a rather binary view on sublime honesty as desirable and ethical. As I reflect on the experience now, I still believe that striving for honesty should be a guiding moral principle where possible, but that ideas of functional collusion and care are helpful for a more nuanced understanding that enables consultants to find ways to go on together because client's anxiety, disappointment, shame and face-saving needs to be taken into account. I could have paid more attention to their feelings of competence and anxiety to explore how we could have compromised in ways to have made it possible to work together. Although I can never know, I think we could have managed to explore the differences in the group.

Project 3: Consultancy and impression management

The narrative in this project involved the top management in the area of health and care for older adults in a large private health care organisation. My assignment involved monthly meetings with the group starting in 2017, and we have worked together since. At one point during spring 2018, Carl, the director, felt under pressure from the board to come up with a clear plan to develop the organisation, and he told us that he wanted the whole organisation to work with 'local cohesion'. He said he wanted the nursing homes and rehabilitation section to cooperate more closely but was not clear about what this meant precisely in their daily practice. I suggested that I could prepare a note about the topic so we could discuss it, and the group of managers agreed. At the subsequent meeting, we engaged in a discussion about 'local cohesion' that Carl quickly interrupted. He was disappointed that the managers had not worked further on the topic. I noticed feelings of shame both in the three managers and me and for not living up to his expectations. Intuitively, I felt reluctant to return to these emotionally intense issues. I feared Carl would be angry with me and perhaps think it was unprofessional of me to draw attention to emotions. I even feared he might end my contract. However, due to my work in Project 2, I was convinced that these emotions were important to explore, so I called Carl to say that I noticed feelings of disappointment and shame and how this might be important to discuss in the group. He agreed, and at the next meeting, I presented my observation. They recognised my experience, and we explored the emotional patterns in our relating. It was as if the air had been cleared, and the rest of the meeting progressed with an easy flow of contributions and discussions as we made plans about how to develop 'local cohesion' in the organisation. We ended the meeting by agreeing that I should make a plan for further work that would sum up our discussions on 'local cohesion'. At the following meeting, I presented the plan, and the managers added that they had launched discussions on the topic in their areas, but Carl interrupted and said that he was getting frustrated again. He needed more action and less conversation. I felt shame again, but I was also irritated that we found ourselves stuck in a pattern of disappointment.

In my reflections on the narrative, I realised that my work with the clients relied on different assumptions with regard to my role as a consultant. My original task involved reflecting *with* them, which was a less controlled approach. That changed when Carl was under pressure, and I tried to live up to his expectations by supporting the creation of a future with more 'local cohesion' as Carl wanted. The latter role relied on the idea that we can create and design the future, as described in early OD literature (e.g., French & Bell, 1995). While Carl was trying to create a future with more 'local cohesion' to impress the board with a strong and clear vision, I tried to create a more positive and harmonious future. In this way, we all seemed to try to control events but failed. I drew on Mead, who convincingly explains how it is impossible to control the future in regard to human relating. We cannot control or predict others' behaviour or how that will affect us in return

(Mead, 1934, p. 7). In Mead's understanding of time, all three tenses coexist because expectations and interpretations of the past influence what happens in the present (Mead, 1932, p. 11). Our anticipations towards the future affect the present and, thereby, how we understand the past, which will change in the future (Mowles, 2011, p. 200). Mowles and Stacey elaborate: 'If this were to apply to an organisation, then decision-making processes that involved forecasting, envisioning future states, or even making any assumptions about future states would be problematic in terms of realising a chosen future' (2016, p. 247). I argued in Project 3 that the future is uncertain and that the ideas of control in change management, process consulting, and OD literature are flawed.

Instead of trying to plan the future, we found ways to explore our patterns of disappointment in the narrative. I found this interesting in relation to my theme of research, and I started to write about the events as a narrative in this thesis. I felt a sense of betrayal about writing about them, though, and I felt obliged to share my reflections with them. I was afraid that they might be angry or think badly of me, but I decided to send the project to them. This served as yet another possibility for us to explore the patterns of relating in the group. Overall, the recurring conversations about disappointment led us to continue our conversations with more curiosity and less blame, and, in that sense, we managed to find ways to bring attention to our patterns of relating with the group. My learning set noticed how my response to Carl's disappointment revealed a need to impress Carl. Their comments made me recognise my need to be perceived as competent and to impress others. It appeared to be a repeating pattern in my practice as a consultant, and I decided to explore this further. I turned to Goffman's (1959) notion of impression management to describe how individuals respond to social norms and rules in order to appear competent in the eyes of others. This led me to focus particularly on what I have experienced as my unconscious need for others to think positively about me as a consultant and how this affects the practice of consultancy.

Reflexive turn

With the insights about consultancy as a political game, I realise how my experienced need to impress Carl and my dependency on his evaluation of my performance is a general aspect of the relationship between consultants and clients. I needed to impress Carl to some degree to keep working with them because I found the work meaningful both content-wise but also financially. In that sense, disappointing clients is the opposite of impressing, and the emotional reactions of disappointment are related to power and the economy within consultancy. Consultants who disappoint clients might lead to contracts being terminated and a threat to their reputation. Impressing clients is part of the political game that enables consultants to get and keep jobs. These dilemmas are the bread and butter of consultancy that are rarely described in the literature, let alone discussed with clients. Critical management studies (CMS) (Alvesson & Willmott, 2002) that I briefly presented in Project 3, addresses issues of dependency and power within consultancy. Alvesson claims that management consultancy operates in the discourse of persuasion to keep 'the client on the hook, keeping him or her happy … using all kinds of methods to secure a personal relationship' (2001, p. 874). CMS draws on critical theory of the Frankfurt tradition to challenge assumptions in management thinking (Alvesson & Willmott, 2003, p. 3). They claim, like I have, that the 'practices and discourses that comprise organizations are never politically neutral' (ibid, p. 16). I agree with the CMS perspective that consultants have intentions, also financial interests, that might be experienced as a pressure to perform and manage the impression they make on clients. Ways to manage one's impression on others are described in detail as impression management in organisational development and management literature, which I will describe in further detail below.

Rosenfeld, Giacalone, and Riordan (1995) describe impression management in organisations as five different tactics (intimidation, exemplification, ingratiation, self-promotion, and supplication). A similar approach is described by Ferris et al. (2005) in relation to political skill as individual capacities (social astuteness, interpersonal influence, networking ability, and apparent sincerity) providing individuals 'the ability to effectively understand others at work, and to use such knowledge to influence others to act in ways that enhance one's personal and/or organizational objectives' (ibid, p. 127). The idea of influence and personal gain through the employment of defined tactics or skills is widely adopted in management journals and described in several areas. The use of impression management tactics has been measured (Bolino & Turnley, 1999), and their use has been correlated with personality traits (Fuller, Barnett, Hester, Relyea, & Frey, 2007). The use of specific impression management tactics is detected and described as particularly prevalent in job employment situations because the stakes are high for the applicant (Rosenfeld, 1997; Weiss & Feldman, 2006). Roberts (2005) takes into account that consultants are under pressure to project an impression of 'competence' (ibid, p. 687) and finds the idea of impression management tactics a useful way to describe how organisational members adapt to these expectations. Harvey et al. (2018) build on Roberts and take the politics of consultancy into account to suggest that tactics 'are far more than just conjuring phony impressions' but are 'a necessary medium' to exercise expertise in consultancy within organisations (ibid, p. 1633). Roberts and Harvey acknowledge that managing one's impression is linked to both social expectations towards consultancy and politics, but in sum, all these authors above instrumentalise impression management into tactics that individuals employ to reach their goals. I recognise my response as 'self-promotion', as one of the impression management-tactic is termed, to get the job in Project 2 and 'ingratiation' towards Carl as another tactic to keep my job in Project 3. However, I did not experience it as isolated tactics that I was choosing in the situation but rather that we were all trying to impress each other in different ways and that our responses and intentions changed as the situation changed. The narrative in Project 3 shows how choosing tactics to impress others is beyond our control and is rather habitual responses tied to our identity, power, and the particular relationships that continuously change. Impression management as a tactical approach primarily describes *how* we try to impress each other, whereas I have become curious towards understanding *why* we try to impress each other and how the attempts to impress others affects processes of organisational development. I will return to explore *why* we try to impress each other in key arguments 2 and 3 and focus on the effects of trying to impress others in processes of organisational development below.

Dale Carnegie's famous text *How to Win Friends and Influence People* published in 1936 (2009) might serve as a starting point for understanding the idea that the deliberate management of the impression one leaves might translate into personal and professional gain. The book has been influential, and I argue that the assumptions behind it are found in the approaches that regard impression management as individual tactics one can employ. The idea of employing techniques to impress others holds individualistic assumptions and instrumentalises ways to think about human interaction as a temporal linear exchange of gestures where one analyses the gesture of the other and responds thereafter. However, it is characteristic for all three of my narratives that everyone was trying to impress others in certain ways and that everybody was aware that they were doing it to some degree. I drew on Mead in Project 3 to describe this as the anticipation of the reaction of the other. Both sides know the game, so to speak, although they may know it more or less consciously.

Clients expect consultants to impress them as competent to some degree although motivations to hire consultants are complex which I will describe further in Key Argument 2 in this synopsis. If they appear too 'confident' and 'in command', it might be experienced as a threat to the manager's position, as Clark & Avakian points out (2013, p. 75). If the performance is too obvious, it might cause suspicion, and if it is experienced as clumsy, it will disappoint clients. Consultants are expected to perform and project an image of themselves as competent while they know that clients are also aware that they are trying to do so. In other words, consultants need to perform in ways that impress clients, knowing that everybody is aware that a game of impression management is being played. The performance of consultancy is obviously more complex than the instrumentalising literature suggests and requires a feel for the game to play it.

This relates to how I have described power as the ongoing negotiation of relational interdependencies particularly in Project 4. I cited Mowles to understand consultants as exercising temporary leadership in ongoing conversations in Project 2 (Mowles, 2009, p. 291). This exercise of leadership relies partly on symbolic power and how consultants impress clients as they interact. Consultants have no formal authority as such, but they are hired by someone with formal authority and their mandate can be withdrawn. So, formal authority is immensely important to the politics of the situation. Carl could have fired me in the narrative. However, as I realised in Project 4 clients and consultants are interdependent; clients are also dependent on the consultant. Carl was dependent on me to help him and his managers out of their stuckness as a group. Inviting consultants into groups is also making clients vulnerable because consultants participate, convince and persuade others as they negotiate themselves into a position of temporary leadership. In short, power is relational whereas authority is tied to a person with an institutional role. This distinction is important because formal responsibility lies with those in authority not necessarily with those in a powerful position. Carl was accountable to the board having formal authority but did not have sufficient power to get his will which might have led to a greater sense of disappointment. This reflexive turn on Project 3 makes me realise that emotional heat in general and disappointment in particular may be heightened when one is in a position of authority but without power.

The conclusion I came to in Project 3 was a departure from the instrumentalising tendency in the management literature and a view of the client-consultant-relationship as interdependent as I pointed out with Elias (1978, p. 78). I have elaborated on this in the above to conclude further how the relationship is not a one-sided aim of getting and keeping the contract where I was dependent on Carl's evaluation of me and in control of the impression I was making. Nor was Carl wholly dependent on me as one who held the key to disturb their stuck relational patterns of disappointment. Although we were interdependent, we were not equal in our interdependency. In key argument 2, I will elaborate further on the subtleties of how consultants and clients need each other and how this plays out as patterns of impressing and disappointing.

Project 4: Power, identity, and ethics in consultancy

In the narrative in Project 4, I described my work with a non-profit organisation for mentally handicapped children. I had worked with them since 2017 through a process where they had expanded their original 'boarding school' with a housing and an occupational department called 'the foundation'. They had formally separated into two organisations with two different CEOs. John was CEO for the foundation, and Peter was CEO for the boarding school. After working as a consultant with management development with both organisations for two years, the boarding school withdrew from further development meetings with the foundation. John kept hiring me to work for the management group in the foundation. Among many other things, John and his managers reflected on a rising critique of 'the school' due to diverging economic interests. This critique culminated with John openly accusing Peter of disloyalty towards the overall purpose at a strategy seminar I facilitated for both boards and management groups. John argued that the school was not supporting the foundation. Peter tried to object that he was constrained by law from supporting the foundation further. John, however, was supported by both boards at the seminar. I believed Peter was making an important argument that we should explore but found myself unable to voice my opinion, which puzzled me.

I had been used to thinking of myself as a helper who facilitated processes where participants are enabled to solve problems in a harmonious atmosphere. I did not succeed with this in the actual situation. Instead, I found myself as an actor in a political game of power struggling to find out which side to take. While I pondered what I should do, Peter had allied with an independent lawyer who supported his arguments. This developed into a visible conflict at our next meeting where neither Peter nor John was willing to change their minds and reach out to the other. I felt their conflict was damaging to the organisations' work for the disabled children and that I should intervene. But I was paralysed, and I felt like a puppet on a string caught in alliances with both Peter and John and that I would disappoint them no matter what I did. My first impulse was to withdraw from the conflict, but I believed that, if I withdrew, it would have negative consequences for the children. I decided to write to them and suggested that the three of us meet. They both declined. John, however, asked me to continue to work with him and his management group. I decided to accept this, which allowed me to continue to explore the ethics of the situation with them.

This led me to explore the conflict as a political game of power. I explored this by drawing on Bourdieu and his concepts: *field, symbolic capital,* and *habitus*. Bourdieu sees power as relationally embedded in specific practices comprised by its actors and their history (2005, p. 206). Symbolic capital is that which is valued and honoured in the field and accumulated by individuals. Habitus is the individually embodied social structure (ibid, p. 216). So, instead of locating conflict in individual needs, I have found Bourdieu useful to understand how our actions and positions were located in broader social structures that change over time. Consultants, as well as managers, need to understand what is valued in the specific field and manage the impression they make, to be influential. This led me to conclude that power struggles are an inherent part of organisational development, and consultants participate as political actors rather than as neutral facilitators. This dawned on me as I realised that either I was supporting the law-bound approach Peter suggested or John's rebellious approach to formal bureaucracy. I also realised that an important part of the politics in the situation relied on the impression I and others were making to persuade John, Peter, their managers, and the board members in order to form alliances.

As I was exploring the situation through the lens of politics and power relations, I was getting less caught up in impressing John and Peter and more concerned about ethics. I felt it was less about me and more about what we were doing together and what the consequences of our actions for everyone involved would be, including the children in the institution. I found Ricoeur's view on ethics and mutual recognition helpful to think about decisions that involved ethics in the narrative. Ricoeur argues that the intention to be helpful and kind is necessary but not sufficient in a particular situation. Ricoeur argues for the notions of *mutual recognition* and *practical wisdom* to guide ethical action (Ricoeur, 2005, p. 88). Mutual recognition is an ethical obligation because 'one cannot be thought of without the other' (Ricoeur, 1992, p. 3), and we can know ourselves only through the recognition of others. Therefore, it is an ethical obligation to make decisions that serve the care of particular others in the specific situation (ibid, p. 262). Care does not mean to soothe others but to take others seriously, which means to listen to them carefully, respond to what they are saying, and let them know what you think. Instrumental positive affirmation of others is, in that sense, the opposite of mutual recognition.

As I was reading Ricoeur, I felt obliged to recognise John and Peter by sharing my reflections from the narrative with them. I felt something was wrong, and I tried to take the 'call' of conscience seriously and return to the clients to explore how I might make sense of it with them. I was afraid that they might be angry with me, but I felt our conversation was more important than what they would think of me. I found the courage to engage in the politics of the situation, and I sent the narrative to them and invited both to meet again. This time individually. They agreed to meet, and I discussed the narrative with both of them, which enabled us to continue to make sense of what we had been doing together. Taking others seriously and acting with care as mutual recognition marked a change in my practice that was characterised by a more honest and outspoken curiosity towards their motives and mine. This changed our work together, my practice as a consultant, and affected me, as well as John and Peter. Ricoeur offers the term 'narrative identity' to understand identity as the dialectic between sameness and otherness where otherness consists of other people, our bodily reactions, and our conscience (1992, p. 140, 2005, p. 91). Personal identity is paradoxically social and individual at the same time, and when consultants help and care for others in the spirit of mutual recognition, they will inevitably change.

Reflexive turn

The first three projects were focused on my experience of being unable to control the impression I was making. In project 4, I realised how others were trying to impress me as well as each other and how impression management was an important part of the politics of any situation. This growing realisation of interdependency in my practice is similar to the interdependency I have experienced as I have conducted this research with my learning set. In the method section, I have dwelt on my reactions as I received their comments, and I have recognised how my research is dependent on them. I have realised with increasing intensity how my learning set colleagues are dependent on me too and have noticed how my commenting has changed in accordance with this realisation in the course of my research. When I started in the learning set, I remember how I was very careful to try not to hurt my colleagues' feelings but eager to impress them with the number of my comments and how clever they would appear. Ricoeur's notion of mutual recognition offers an important concept to understand how my commenting has developed similarly to my practice as a consultant; from an eagerness to impress to giving an account of how I react to our work together, an invitation to discuss our reactions and a willingness to make reparations if I cause harm. I am trying to pay more attention to how my actions affect and have consequences for others and how others are affecting each other.

Since writing Project 4, I am experiencing how this relational focus has led to engagement and exploration with others about what we are doing rather than positively affirming and thereby passing judgments on oneself and others. This represents a different quality, that of mutual recognition. I owe my understanding of recognition to both Ricoeur (1992, 2005) and Honneth (2003). Ricoeur acknowledges his debt to Honneth, although, in contrast to Honneth, he does not see recognition exclusively as a struggle but also as a more peaceful experience (Ricoeur, 2005, p. 186). I agree with Ricoeur that recognition can be both. In Project 2 and in the DMan community, I was struggling to be recognised as good enough, whereas my relationships with the groups of managers in Projects 3 and 4 and my colleagues in the DMan community have developed into close relationships. They even resemble friendships as it is described by Ricoeur. He describes friendships as characterised by its contribution to one's sense of self 'without taking anything away' (1992, p. 188). Ricoeur argues that it is through friendship that we experience the irreplaceability of the other. 'In this respect, it is experiencing the irreparable loss of the loved other that we learn, through the transfer of the other onto ourselves, the irreplaceable nature of our own life' (ibid, p. 193). It is unusual to use words such as friendship, care, and love in relation to consultancy within organisational development, but as I reflect on Project 4, I experience that the long history and close relationship between John and Peter had been fruitful and productive over the years but also complicated their conflict emotionally, which affected us all. I have developed close relationships with the groups of managers in Projects 3 and 4 as well as with my colleagues in the DMan community. I have noticed that friendships and even marital relationships evolve in groups I work with. When I am hired to work with conflicts in groups, they always involve personal relationships, likes, and dislikes between people and give rise to fantasies about who is talking with whom both inside and outside of the formal time and space of the organisation. Most organisations have rules about how spouses are not allowed to work in the same unit or that you cannot hire close family members, yet this does not cover the complexity of how close relations and friendships evolve in organisations, and its impact on the work is rarely discussed. Perhaps this is the case because it stands in stark contrast to that of being professionals with expert knowledge, as Clark & Avakian describes organisational development (OD) (2013, p. 26). However, I will argue that friendship and care are inherent parts of human relating that are not restricted by the boundaries of organisations. Ricoeur's notion of mutual recognition might provide a more nuanced vocabulary to think about close relationships in organisations.

Key arguments

In the following section, I have set out three arguments in which I sum up, elaborate, and substantiate my main arguments to address my research question: *How does the pressure to perform and impress others affect consultancy in organisational development?* The research has been conducted from my perspective as a consultant within organisational development, working primarily in public organisations in Denmark, and the arguments are addressed in relation to this practice.

1. I argue that consultants within organisational development are under pressure to perform and manage the impression they make to appear in control of the direction of the development, future outcomes, and the positive mindset of oneself and others. Getting positive affirmation is important for consultants to think of themselves as successful, and the inevitable emergence of disappointment is not only experienced as a threat to their contracts but also to their sense of competence and identity. This hinders important reflections about what we are doing in our work practices and why we are doing it.

2. Impression management is entangled with the politics of consultancy. Consultants are caught up in power relations and the politics of organisational life along with their clients. Consultants are not neutral as helpers but are interdependent political actors with a specific history and intentions. Consultants and clients are interdependent, although the interdependency is unequal because consultants and clients need each other for different reasons at different times. This means that consultants have to impress clients to appear competent while knowing that everybody might be aware that a game of impression management is being played. Reflexive exploration of one's need to impress can be a way to explore power relations.

3. Impressing clients expresses consultants' identity as their self-constancy over time. *Self-constancy is vital to our sense of identity and our capacity to act ethically.* The pressure to impress challenges this idea of self-constancy because consultants might become caught up in the need to impress others which might distract them from focusing on ethics. Consultancy requires the courage to take a position, although it can lead to exclusion. Taking clients seriously in the spirit of mutual recognition and care means to take a position and yet be curious and open to change this position at the same time. Reflexive inquiry enables consultants to focus more intensely on ethics in the particular situation.

I will explain the arguments in detail below.

Argument 1: Consultants experience a need to impress their clients due to a relational, rather than merely individual, pressure to perform

My first argument is that

> *Consultants within organisational development are under pressure to perform and are paradoxically cocreating this pressure on themselves and others - this arises partly as a consequence of our individualised times. The inevitable emergence of disappointment is not only experienced as a threat to their contracts but also to their sense of competence and identity, which might hinder important reflections about what we are doing and why we are doing it.*

It is common to think of performance as an achievement and doing a task well. This understanding of performance is found in the popular notion of 'performance management' in organisational work and originates from 'scientific management' coined by Frederik Taylor. Performance management entails that organisational performance is improved through controlling individual behaviour (Armstrong, 2009, p. 27; Ashdown, 2018, p. 8). The key ingredient is the alignment of individuals' performance to preset organisational goals and expressed expectations (Ashdown, 2018, p. 5). Instead of thinking about performance as an individual achievement, I have found Goffman's dramaturgical metaphor more relevant to describe consultancy as a performance in which individuals respond to norms and rules to come across as competent in social situations (1959). This is close to Mead's understanding of how we respond to social objects (Mead, 1925, pp. 265–266), in this case, the social object of consultancy within organisational development. I argued in Project 3, under the influence of Mead, that to go beyond understanding behaviour as an individual response to fixed norms, we need to think of interaction as gesturing and responding that continually form both individuals and social objects. The latter understanding has similarities with Butler's notion of performativity, as Hodgson has applied it to organisational work. This view describes performances as processual and thereby 'suggests a way in which identity may be similarly seen as constructed in and through conduct rather than as *pre-existing* conduct' (Hodgson, 2005, p. 54 italics in original). This means that the performance of consultants is shaping and being shaped by the social object of consultancy, the group's expectations of what a consultant should be doing, within organisational development at the same time. Elias emphasises a similar view where individuals are interdependent, and a relational approach to impression management means to explore why it is important for everyone that consultants perform, impress, and be positively affirmed as a consultant within organisational development.

In Project 2, I draw on Elias to explain how the striving to stand out as autonomous individuals, termed as individualism (2001, pp. 141–142), is important to understand in relation to the experienced need to impress others as competent. I argue that an important influence on the social object of consultancy within organisational development is this influence from individualism. Influential authors across different disciplines such as philosophy (e.g., Han, 2015; Taylor, 1991), sociology (e.g., Sennett, 1998, 2007), and psychology (e.g., Brinkmann, 2017, 2019) point similarly to problems associated with the idea that individuals are entrepreneurial selves caught up in self-improvement. Ehrenreich (2010, p. 51) describes how individualism involves an inflated sense of agency and argues further how individualism is closely linked to positive thinking in the context of organisational work. This view is elaborated further by Cabanas and Illouz (2019) who critique the view that individuals are thought to be 'free, strategic, responsible and autonomous beings who are able to govern their psychological states at will, fulfil their interests and pursue what is understood to be their inherent objective in life: the achievement of their own happiness' (ibid, p. 51). This is vividly debated in Denmark where Brinkmann is a prominent proponent for a sceptical view on the individualising tendencies and links this to self-criticism: 'The message is that everything is possible if you believe in it enough and want it enough. If things don't work out, it's because you haven't mobilized enough will and motivation. One consequence of this is that you automatically criticize yourself when something is problematic: you internalize external social critique and transform it into inner self-criticism' (Brinkmann, 2017, p. 78). I am not arguing that individualism is a problem in itself, as Taylor also points out (1991, pp. 2–3), but it might be experienced as a pressure on individuals to perform in ways where consultants appear in control of future outcomes and the positive mindset of oneself and others and where positive affirmation is the currency to evaluate whether one is successful in doing so.

I experienced the need to impress as an individual as a natural given, but it is rather history turned into nature, to use Bourdieu's phrasing (1977, p. 78). Individuals' experience of a need for positive affirmation are ripples that shape and are shaped by the deeper currents of individualising tendencies. So, instead of an individual *need*, I will describe my incentive to impress as a relational *pressure*, that is, created in relationships with others rather than as internal mechanisms. Responses to the pressure to impress have been expressed as competition, disappointment, stress, doubt, pride, withdrawal, and guilt in this thesis. The narratives in this thesis take place in the specific context of the field of public sector work in Denmark, and the responses to the pressure to impress will differ for other fields of work in other countries. This will be influenced by social differences and inequalities created by race, class, and gender, as examples. During this research, I have become particularly aware of gender in relation to my theme of research. For example, Scharff had interviewed self-employed female musicians and their experiences of balancing between self-promotion and typical feminine prescriptions to be modest, helpful, and supportive (2015, p. 103). In contrast, it is often the case that men experience a pressure to express ambition and to compete, especially in the public domain (Benschop, van den Brink, Doorewaard, & Leenders, 2013, p. 703). I have explored literature on gender (Alvesson & Billing, 1997; Sullivan, 2000) that makes the argument that gender differences are embedded in our habits. I find that this was the case when I tried to solve problems as a manager in Project 1 in solitude. It was a response to the invitation to act as a stereotypical lonely male hero. These variations in responses display the gendered quality of the pressure to impress.

I argue that impression management is a social and relational process, which is in contrast to the predominant view in management literature where it is described as instrumental skills or tactics that individuals can employ to meet their goals (Rosenfeld et al., 1995). I claim that one of the problems with impression management as a tactical approach is that it locates abilities in the individual. I experienced this problem as a breakdown when I tried to overcome challenges I faced with the acquisition of individual complexity competencies as described in Projects 1 and 3. The pursuit of perfecting individual tactics, skills, abilities, or competencies amplified, rather than solved, the breakdowns in these projects. Locating the ability to impress others in individuals might take the shape of competition because being recognised and doing well involves, at least in part, comparing oneself to others, particularly in relation to the manager who employs the consultant. In that sense, disappointment is the opposite of impressing, and getting caught up in either impressing or disappointing others distract one from focusing on the relational character of the work as a consultant. It is giving the illusion that organisational development relies on individual's skills and performances, whereas it is always both individual and social.

I argue that emotions are embodied expressions with cultural and social meanings (Burkitt, 1999; Wetherell, 2012) and disappointment is important in organisational work. Positive expectations always hold the potential for disappointment. Hence, I argue that it is important for consultants within organisational development to pay attention to their own as well as participant's emotions and bodily reactions. Emotions should not be process-reduced, from Elias, into a state or an entity inside individuals (1978, p. 112). Burkitt elaborates on emotions as relational and embodied with Bourdieu: *'thought is not structured by anything that could be considered as a mind which is somehow distinct from the body, whether this is a set of cognitive structures or categories, or innate ideas. Instead, it is acquired bodily actions or habits that make thought possible'* (Burkitt, 1999, p. 76 italics in original). This means that understanding is 'a practical process—a way of being-in-the-world through embodied activity rather than cognitive reflection' (ibid, p. 87). I argue further that Ricoeur's description of our own bodies as otherness (1992, p. 319) is helpful for accepting that consultants or clients are not in control of their bodily reactions but might inquire into them together to explore what they express. Being dependent on positive affirmation might make one fail to pay attention to the relational aspect of emotions and withdraw from an exploration of emotions due to feelings of disappointment and shame.

Argument 2: Impressing clients in particular ways is an inevitable part of the politics of consultancy within organisational development because consultants are not neutral actors

My second argument is that

Impression management is entangled with the politics of consultancy. Consultants are caught up in power relations and the politics of organisational life along with their clients, and they perform and impress clients in certain ways to appear competent. This means that consultants have to impress clients to appear competent while knowing that everybody might be aware that a game of impression management is being played. Reflexive exploration of one's experienced need to impress can be a way to explore power relations.

In this argument, I claim that the way consultants perform and wish to impress clients is influenced by the politics of the specific situation. Power and politics are usually not paid attention to as key concepts in dominant literature on management, and organisations are rather thought of as harmonious systems, according to Clegg (2006) and Fleming & Spicer (2014). I build on Elias's processual sociology (1978) and Bourdieu's understanding of power (2005) to claim that power is not a thing or a possession but relational dependencies that might be characterised by both conflict and harmony. Consultants and clients are interdependent, although they need each other for different reasons and to different extents. The dependency shifts during the course of a consultancy task, and the way we perform and impress each other changes accordingly. I will briefly describe key parts of my work as a consultant to point out how consultants' performance and need to impress clients are intertwined with power during the flow of a task.

Clients always have expectations when they contact me to hear about prospects of working together. I try to understand their expectations to find out whether I can help them and, at the same time, try to project an image of myself as credible and competent for the job so they will choose to work with me if I think I can help them. The consultant is dependent on the client to choose them over other consultants. Consultancy is political from the very start because it involves the effort of trying to promote interests and influence others. In Project 2, I tried to impress the group and convince them to hire me by bringing my book into the conversation to appear credible. However, some members of the group felt anxious about whether they were good enough, I later discovered. This highlights how consultants are always outsiders needing to impress even though they are foreign to the organisation. Consultants have to learn and build credibility fast (Bourgoin & Harvey, 2018). Impression management is important to project an image of oneself as useful and competent to be able to work together with clients.

Once a contract is made, it contains deliverables. I have described longer termed tasks in Projects 3 and 4, which involved presenting theory, reflecting with groups of managers, and facilitating planned processes with larger groups. Sometimes, I only give one lecture for a group of people, but most often, I have longer-term work with groups of managers or employees where my task consists of teaching, helping, and reflecting. It involves finding consensus and harmony as well as provoking critical thinking. The politics of the situation becomes obvious when differences in interests emerge. This puts pressure on consultants to take sides, which is related to power. In Project 3, I found myself taking Carl's side at moments and his manager's side at other moments. When I asked for Carl's permission to share my experience of disappointment with the group, I also placed him in a position to decide. These were acts intended to leave an impression of me as a loyal helper to him as a response to the politics of the situation. I was afraid he would be disappointed with me if I brought up these issues without his approval. Disappointing clients is, to some extent, the opposite of impressing and a threat to contracts and consultants' reputations, as I described in the reflexive turn on Project 3.

In Project 4, I was dependent on John for recognition and potentially more work but found myself siding with Peter in terms of the argument. It entailed the risk of exclusion to take the 'call' of conscience seriously and go back to them. In Project 4, I was name-dropping Elias to the clients, which is a typical way to impress. It might serve as a safe way to approach difficult relational subjects with clients. However, it might also create a distance to the topic at hand where it is easily dismissed despite (or perhaps because) its relevance, as I believe was the case in Project 4. Besides, this might silence people because they fear appearing incompetent, as happened in Project 2. Consultants impressing too much might make managers or their staff dependent on the consultant and thereby threaten and undermine the manager's position of power. Consultants may be experienced as a threat to management if they appear too competent (Clark & Avakian, 2013, p. 75). Presenting oneself as a researcher draws on the same symbolic capital of intellectual affiliation and might have the same side effects as name-dropping. The ways consultants perform and impress clients in the micro interactions, as described in the narratives, is vital to understanding consultancy within organisational development. This requires careful attention to how the bodies are placed in a room, how the particular gesturing is performed, the tone of voices, eye contact, and the detail of turn-taking in conversations. Having the power to decide the order of speakers, the length of their contribution, and referring to what others have said are all means of managing the impression consultants make on clients that are related to the politics of the situation. Consultants and clients are interdependent as political actors, and the economy of consultancy shapes, and is shaped by, the specific ways consultants and clients impress each other. Generally, consultants need to pay attention to the details of the symbols of competency—understood as the symbolic capital in the field (Bourdieu, 2005, pp. 206–207)—in the specific organisation. This encompasses how people use the latest jargon from management theory, dress to match the informal dress code, produce elegant PowerPoint slides (Stein, 2017, p. 112), speak with confidence and certainty, present and communicate with skill (Smith, 2008, p. 226), reveal personal stories, and show emotions adjusted to the emotional habitus of the organisation.

The constitution of symbolic capital varies for different organisations, so I am not suggesting generic tools to decode a field and behave accordingly. Consultancy requires a feel for the game, which is always in relation to the particular situation. For example, in Project 4, I described how John and Peter were unable to advocate economic growth because it had less symbolic capital than the welfare of the disabled children. Another area of tension that I described included the difficulty of voicing critique or negative emotions under the influence of positive thinking (Alvesson & Willmott, 2002; Cabanas & Illouz, 2019; Clancy et al., 2012; Ehrenreich, 2010; Fineman, 2006). With these critics of positive thinking, I argue that consultants need to take account of the expectations to create a positive atmosphere in the way they perform because they are dependent on the clients to get and keep jobs.

Attempts to impress others might spark suspicion if we come across as insincere. As examples, I became suspicious of Anna's motives when she affirmed me in Project 2, and John and Peter became suspicious of each other in Project 4. Organisational development is a performance, in Goffman's terms, where we all play parts as we interact with others. 'People who play a part are potentially unreliable, because they have more than one face they can display' (Runciman, 2018, p. 8). Both clients and consultants are more or less consciously aware of the performative character of the situation in which consultants are performing to impress as competent while knowing that clients are probably aware that a game of impression management is being played. Consultants are, to varying degrees, expected to avoid disappointing and arousing suspicion in clients to act in accordance with the social object of consultancy within organisational development.

Consultants might try to give the impression of themselves as neutral individuals helping from a position outside of the organisation. As Clark & Avakian presents OD, 'At the heart of the OD literature is the portrayal of the consultant as a professional helper who is drawing on an expert body of knowledge that clients inherently recognize and value' (2013, p. 26). This position might be unassailable until conflicts become visible, and neutrality is impossible, as described in Project 4. The idea of organisations and individuals as systems has been predominant in Danish practice and literature on consultancy within organisational development (Haslebo & Nielsen, 2000; Haslebo, 2004, p. 17; Schnoor & Jack, 2020, p. 15) over the last 30 years. The awareness that each consultancy task sits in a specific field with a history of specific relations and expectations where the consultant is a participant with intentions that affect their work is absent or underemphasised in these approaches. Throughout this thesis I have described how consultants have an interest in presenting themselves as neutral helpers that support clients' needs. I have argued that it is impossible to be neutral due to the politics of the situation. One might argue, from a social constructionist view, that neutrality is socially constructed as a rhetorical manoeuvre and that being neutral is a matter of perspective. However, I refer specifically to the politics in the context of organisational development where claims for neutrality is related to power and the politics of the situation and is not only a matter of perspective. I have argued that consultants that are claiming neutrality cover over the power relations by doing so and is rather an impression that consultants may wish to leave in order to form alliances with those in positions of power. I will claim that positioning oneself as a neutral helper is one way for consultants to manage the impression they make in the political game of power. I agree that consultants should help clients, but I am drawing attention to how the idea of helping does not take heed of the complexity involved. Presenting oneself simply as a helper is aimed at persuasion, which glosses over the complexity and covers over the power negotiations that are involved.

Scholars in the critical management studies tradition (CMS) have helpfully pointed out how consultants are in the discourse of persuasion to get 'the client on the hook…' (2001, p. 874). This might lead consultants to over-selling promises as seen in one large Danish management consultancy agency when they claimed in an advertisement about a year ago: 'Problems can be complicated - solutions cannot'[2]. From the perspective of CMS, advertisements such as this probably appear as mere persuasion. Consultants who are over-selling promises display the instrumentalisation within orthodox management literature and might offer hope to clients, as I quoted Mowles to suggest in Project 3 (2015, p. 48) but also capitalise on the need for certainty in uncertain situations. Stein has coined this as

---

[2] https://implementconsultinggroup.com/problems-can-be-complicated-solutions-cannot/

'profitable uncertainty' to describe the uncertainty that the business of management consultancy targets in order to sell their services (2017, p. 170). I have been particularly influenced by the perspective of complex responsive processes of relating's inspiration from the sociologists Elias and Bourdieu to explore how performance and impression management are related to norms and power in organisations. I differ from critical management studies' one-sided view on consultants as 'virtuosos in symbolic manipulation' (Jackall in Clark & Salaman, 1998, p. 22) and critical management scholars' clearly expressed aim to create emancipatory change through bringing power out as an explicit characteristic (Alvesson & Willmott, 2003, p. 17). I agree with the perspective from CMS that consultants are dependent on the client's perception of them as competent to keep working for them, but I have found literature that highlights the client-consultant relation as interdependent more relevant to explain the events in the narratives. Clients are also dependent on consultants to support their position of power, to be affiliated with their credibility as researchers or authors, to make use of their experience, to draw attention to and disrupt stuck patterns of relating to lead them out of their impasse as described in Project 3. Just being outsiders and new to groups makes a difference from the usual dynamics in groups and offers opportunities for clients to take a more detached view of themselves. The narratives reveal how both clients and consultants are aware of the interdependency in the relationship and have the reflexive capacity to act on it. I agree with Vine as he argues that a 'sensitivity to nuance, complexity and paradox has the potential to help us better understand agency' (2020, p. 478).

I am suggesting a view of the client-consultant relationship in which managing impressions is one way to be influential, although it is not solely within the consultant's control to get the client on the hook, to get affirmation as competent, or to disturb and disrupt clients' stuck patterns of interacting with each other. Clark and Avakian describes this as a view on client-consultant relationships where one 'recognizes mutual insecurities and pressures and leads to a more nuanced understanding of the micro-practices and existential factors that create, sustain, undermine and rebuild control by both parties' (2013, p. 76). They point to a need for research that understands the client-consultant relationship from this nuanced and dynamic view (ibid, p. 78). I have tried to make a contribution to this understanding in relation to the experience of the pressure to impress where consultants and clients are interdependent, as I argued drawing on Elias, although not equal in their interdependence. Consultancy entails continuous negotiations of the interdependencies. Developing one's awareness as a political actor allows consultants to 'become more aware of the patterns of relating that prevail, thus potentially improving one's ability to decide skilfully when to play the game and when to challenge it' (Curtis, 2018, p. 141). I drew on Bourdieu to highlight whether one understands the field and has sufficient symbolic power in a situation to disrupt the functional collusion. Failing to be careful about symbolic capital might lead to rejection of consultants and termination of contracts. Consultants act into the competing politics in the specific situation with groups of clients having diverging intentions and where the consultants have intentions of their own—professionally, ethically, and financially. Impressing clients in particular ways is an inevitable part of the politics of consultancy within organisational development.

The reflexive exploration of one's experience of disappointment and need to impress is a way to explore power relations. Reflexive inquiry allows for detachment and decentring from the individually felt emotional experience to explore how it is related to power relations in the particular group. This requires curiosity and suspicion, as I described with Josselson (2004) in Project 4, and involves a persistent exploration of emotions. This might be unsettling and destabilising because reflexivity entails the effort of enduring 'mental unrest' as I quoted Dewey to say earlier in this synopsis (1910, p. 12). Avoiding exploring the 'mental unrest' might lead consultants to be too caught up in individually felt emotions of disappointment and deflect attention to the power negotiations that are going on. Reflexive exploration allows consultants to pay attention to how consultants are not the only ones trying to impress others and how this is related to power. In Project 4, I argued that this attention is cultivated in consultancy with inspiration from anthropological and sociological research approaches by thinking about what is valued in the specific organisation and who benefits from the work.

This has allowed me to understand how Carl, John, and Peter were not only trying to impress me but also their boards, which affected what we were doing together. Reflexive exploration can be exercised with clients to discuss emotions and power relations and to question functional colluding, as described in Project 3. It requires a feel for the game but also courage, as I described in Project 4 because consultants face the risk of exclusion, which might also be experienced as a threat to one's identity. Being concerned about how others think about one as a consultant is more than a response to the invitation to perform as an individual and more than increasing one's influence in political games of power. Identity and ethics are important reasons to understand why we manage the impression we make in others. This brings me to the third and final argument, which is about how the experience of a need to impress as a consultant is linked to identity and ethics.

Argument 3: Impressing clients in an ethical way requires self-constancy, taking a position and yet being open to change this position at the same time

My third argument is that

> *Impressing clients expresses consultants' identity as their self-constancy over time. Self-constancy is vital to our sense of identity and our capacity to act ethically. The pressure to impress challenges this idea of self-constancy because consultants might be caught up in the need to impress others. Taking clients seriously in the spirit of mutual recognition and care means to take a position and yet being curious and open to change this position at the same time.*

Impressing clients in an ethical way requires self-constancy and taking a position so that clients can develop a sense of who the consultant is and what they stand for. Brinkmann (2017), Sennett (1998), Stein (2017), and Han (2015) have described how the idea of self-improvement as a historical phenomenon places individuals under pressure to be flexible, adaptable, and positive. This might lead to stress, burn-out, exhaustion, fatigue, and depression. Brinkmann has highlighted the need to focus on self-constancy to counter this pressure (2017). This is relevant for consultants who are continuously under pressure to impress clients so they, the consultants, can get and keep jobs while they also face the potential of being lost in their need for positive affirmation. Getting caught up in trying to impress might draw consultants away from what they stand for. I have drawn on Ricoeur's work to argue that being responsible as a consultant means to be recognisable as the same person over time so that clients can count on them.

> Self-constancy is for each person that manner of conducting himself or herself so that others can *count on* that person. Because someone is counting on me, I am *accountable for* my actions before another. The term "responsibility" unites both meanings: "counting on" and "being accountable for" (Ricoeur, 1992, p. 165 italics in original).

In the context of consultancy, I argue that self-constancy means to be constant across working with people and across time so that clients know who the consultant is as an individual and in relation to them. The impression consultants make on clients is an expression of who they are and what clients can expect from them. Clients need to know consultants to trust and count on them as they work together. Brinkmann explains how Ricoeur views self-constancy as a precondition for counting on each other and thereby also for being ethical. 'We can only make promises and commit to actions together over time because we understand ourselves as being the same over time—because we have a more or less coherent identity … only individuals with self-constancy feel guilt and are capable of being moral' (2017, pp. 107–108). Self-constancy is vital to our sense of identity, to our capacity to act ethically, and to make and keep promises to others. This entails, drawing on Ricoeur (1992, p. 295), the need among consultants to pay careful attention to how their identity and intentions have been shaped because this influences their actions and has consequences for others. We do not have complete access to how we are shaped and how that affects us, so we do not always know why we wish to leave a certain impression on others. The ethics involved in mutual recognition imply that consultants should strive to reflexively explore their identity and give an account of themselves to clients.

Care in the spirit of mutual recognition means to be honest and courageous in taking a position and speaking from this position. Care is not to be mistaken for automated or instrumentalised positive affirmation. 'An ethic of care may sometimes dictate taking difficult, hard and unpleasant actions in support of a person, an institution or even a thing one cares for' (Vince & Gabriel, 2011, p. 11). I have critiqued how appreciative inquiry invites consultants to support a harmonious atmosphere and avoid open conflicts. I have argued that to care for others means taking others seriously, which is not necessarily experienced as harmony or as helpful to clients. To care for others means to be curious and this requires courage because it might lead to conflict, exclusion, and loss of contracts, as described in Project 4. I have drawn on authors who view diverging opinions, critique, and conflict as inherent parts of politics (Clegg, 2006, p. 847; Fleming & Spicer, 2014, p. 239; Ricoeur, 1992, p. 258). Critique from this perspective is not intrinsically good or bad (Messner, Clegg, & Kornberger, 2008, p. 69), and politics is not seen as a nuisance to everyday practice in organisations (Fleming & Spicer, 2014, p. 240). I agree with Solso as she argues for a more optimistic view of conflicts (Solso, 2016, p. 176). Being stuck in long-term patterns of conflict is problematic, but the unsettling experience as we encounter difference and conflict might also offer ways to sustain openness and reflexively inquire into power relations, ethics, and identity.

I argue that the way consultants impress clients expresses their identity, and I have drawn on Ricoeur to argue that mutual recognition and care involves an ethical obligation to take a position. I am not suggesting an ideal of the self as constant and unchangeable though. Taylor criticises such an ideal, lending itself to individualised accounts of an inner authentic self (1991, p. 29). I agree with Taylor's understanding of the self as relational, one that is authentic in its obligations to others and to oneself. Mutual recognition implies that consultants listen to clients and take them seriously in ways that might lead to change and a disruption of one's self-constancy. We are bound to change when we take other people, our bodily reactions, and the 'call' of conscience seriously (Ricoeur, 1992, p. 140, 2005, p. 91). Ricoeur's notion of narrative identity entails the dialectic between sameness and otherness where we paradoxically are the same and yet continually change (1992, p. 140). Paradoxes are not to be solved, resolved or dissolved but holds a pedagogical potential for a more nuanced understanding of practice (Vine, 2020, p. 478). This particular paradox enables consultants to think about organisational change as identity change for consultants as well as for clients. This is different from pervasive ideas about consultancy—the social object of consultancy, as explained in Project 3—where consultants are expected to facilitate change for the clients. Consultancy requires the courage to be open to change in the face of otherness, although this might be experienced as a threat to one's sense of self and a loss of identity (Ricoeur, 1992, pp. 149–150). We are other to ourselves, hence Ricoeur's expression and title of his book, *Oneself as Another* (1992). I find that this threat is described eloquently by Dewey as perplexity, hesitation, and doubt. I argue, with Dewey, that it is important to engage in reflective thinking as a consultant, which requires enduring and curiously exploring the mental unrest because it reveals one's thinking (1910, p. 12). For example, I was emotionally distressed when my approach to consultancy was questioned in Project 2. My default response was to put effort into impressing the clients as competent, which some experienced as pressure. So, my effort to impress others had consequences for them; they felt incompetent and silenced. I ended up doubting whether I was competent as a consultant due to the rejection in Project 2. Locating disappointment within individuals might blind consultants towards what is happening relationally, politically, and ethically. With the help from my research colleagues, I managed to endure the anxiety and return to the clients in Project 3 to share my feelings of disappointment. In Project 4, I found the courage to return to the clients and explore the ethics of the situation with them despite the risk of disappointment, rejection, and exclusion. I realised how we were all trying to impress each other and how this was expressing power relations; John and Peter were trying to impress both the board, and me as a consultant who might have influence, to build alliances.

Consultants as well as clients might find themselves caught up in trying to impress each other which might distract them from focusing on ethics. Focusing on research and reflexive inquiry rather than impressing others enables consultants to focus more intensely on both power and ethics in the particular situation. Sharing the narratives in this thesis with Carl, Peter, and John were difficult situations, but also led to vital conversations that enabled us to explore what we were doing and to move on together. I was taking a clear position to insist on exploring the ethics of the situation with Peter and John. This is not to say that I rigidly followed a moral rule or took a stand that I was not prepared to back down from. I agree with the general moral rule that people should help others but argue that the notion of a helper is not sufficient to guide actions in practice. For example, helping John in Project 4 would disadvantage Peter and vice versa. Universal moral rules such as 'do no harm', 'love your neighbour', and 'help others' are necessary but not sufficient to guide consultants in their practice. Ethical decisions cannot rely on moral rules alone but are guided by practical wisdom where the notion of care for the particular other offers ways to reflect, discuss, and act in the particular situation. It requires the exercise of practical wisdom in the specific situation to decide whether to take a position or, in rare cases, an ultimate stand. The consequences of our actions will always be unpredictable, which is why the exercise of practical wisdom is ongoing in relationships. We need to pay attention to the consequences for others and be prepared to continue the conversation and make reparations if necessary.

I argued in Project 4, with Ricoeur, that aiming for the good life with and for others requires mutual recognition as an ethical obligation. Ricoeur, as a hermeneutical thinker, acknowledges how his own thinking is historically embedded and does not provide a universal code of ethics. His thinking is contextual (1992, p. 287). He is merely pointing to how one cannot be thought of without the other, from the Hegelian position, and then suggesting mutual recognition to guide actions in the particular situation. In my understanding this is why he humbly terms his theory of ethics as 'little ethics' implying that there is no all-encompassing ethical theory to be put forward (ibid, p. 290). I will repeat the following quote to emphasise my argument that ethical action relies on the ongoing discussion with others. 'In this regard, one of the faces of practical wisdom ... is the art of conversation, in which the ethics of argumentation is put to the test in the conflict of convictions' (Ricoeur, 1992, p. 290). This has led me to argue that to impress others in ethical ways in processes of organisational change consultants are obliged to take a position. Consultants are responsible for attempting to give an honest account of their convictions and they bear the responsibility to insist that those they work with do the same to accommodate an ongoing debate. Self-constancy is required in order to take a position while open-mindedness is required when trying to take account of plural moral responses.

Ethics emerged as a theme in the narratives in Project 3 and more clearly in Project 4. The problem-driven approach I have employed means that I did not plan to take ethics up from the beginning. The idea of problem-driven research is to explore problems and breakdowns to find new ways to think about the problem. In that sense, the themes chose me instead. I have described how consultants are expected to perform and impress as competent which implies the imminent risk of getting lost in oneself. On this backdrop, Ricoeur is relevant because he has developed ideas about how ethics is linked to self-constancy which is generative for thinking about the problems that emerged in new ways.

To conclude this third argument, I claim that impressing clients in ethical ways requires self-constancy which means to take a position as a consultant. However, acting ethically in the spirit of mutual recognition means, paradoxically, to be open to identity change at the same time. This is linked to identity and might arouse strong emotions. Reflexive exploration into these emotions is important to avoid being too caught up in impressing others which might deflect attention to the ethics of the situation. Ethical decisions rely on moral rules and care for the particular other in the specific situation.

Contributions of this thesis

My research makes a general contribution to literature about how impressing and disappointing others is related to emotions, power, identity, and ethics in consultancy within organisational development. Impression management is entangled with the political and financial economy of consultancy, expresses our identity, and entails the responsibility of taking a position and accounting for oneself towards others (as well as to oneself) and the obligation to listen to clients, which will lead to change in oneself. In the following paragraphs I will describe the contributions in relation to knowledge and practice in further detail. But first I will dwell on how these contributions have arisen from the narratives and the explorations into my practice as a self-employed consultant working primarily in public organisations in Denmark. Based on the auto-ethnographical accounts, the analysis in the projects and the synopsis, my experience as both manager and consultant and the literature I am confident that the contributions above are generalisable warranted assertions for consultants within organisational development in the Danish public sector. I frequently work in the private sector too, but I am less confident about the applicability in this area since the narratives are not derived from this context. The auto-ethnographical approach I have employed brings out the detail of the interactions in the specific context but has limitations with regard to generalisability beyond this context. Therefore, I also acknowledge the differences and diversity among consultants that derive from geography, consultant's culture and individual history, gender and class which limit the generalisability of the contributions.

Contribution to knowledge

First, I claim that the pressure to perform and manage the impression one makes is generalisable for consultants in organisational development more generally. It is described in literature across the disciplines of sociology (e.g., Goffman, 1959), anthropology (e.g., Stein, 2017), management theory (e.g., Rosenfeld et al., 1995), and critical management studies (e.g., Alvesson, 2001), albeit with fundamentally different approaches and explanations. Consultants are under pressure to impress due to the temporary relationship with clients, and this is amplified by broader tendencies of individualism, which might be experienced as an individual need to impress. It is well described in management literature *how* we manage the impression we make on others (Rosenfeld et al., 1995). My research contributes by offering a description and analysis of *why* consultants manage the impression they make and how this is related to power, identity, and ethics within consultancy in the Danish public sector.

Second, I have drawn on different disciplines (primarily anthropology, sociology, and philosophy) to explain how consultancy has relatively recently become more rooted in ideas about individualism and positive thinking (Cabanas & Illouz, 2019; Ehrenreich, 2010) and how positive affirmation is important for consultants to think of themselves as standing out as successful individuals. Positive affirmation is linked to power in the sense that consultants might find themselves dependent on positive affirmation. The inevitable emergence of disappointment is often experienced as a threat to consultants' contracts as well as their sense of competence and identity, whereby the engagement with negative emotions are avoided. This might hinder important reflections about what we are doing and why we are doing it, particularly in relation to power and ethics.

Third, I have contributed to the understanding of how impression management plays out as local interactions between interdependent individuals in organisations. Consultants and clients are interdependent, but their interdependencies are unequal due to the specific power relations of the situation. Consultants and clients need each other, but for different reasons. Consultants are political actors in games of power, and it is important for them to perform and impress clients. The exploration of my experience of a need to impress has contributed to knowledge about why consultants perform to impress, how they do it, and what the consequences might be. Consultants might promise tools and techniques to provide hope and relieve the anxiety that uncertainty entails. Consultants might affirm clients instrumentally and support clients in positions of power in the micro-processes of turn-taking and in informal conversations. Consultants might present themselves as neutral helpers, experts, or researchers. I have contributed with descriptions of how these gestures also have the potential to lead to disappointment, shame, and suspicion, which might lead to both consultants and clients experiencing competition, loneliness, stress, failure, and feeling not good enough. The specific responses to the pressure to perform and the motivation for impression management for the individual consultant are multiple, many layered and changeable as I have pointed out in the beginning of this paragraph.

Fourth, emotions have been described extensively in the literature on organisations. My particular contribution has been to focus on the role of emotions in the client-consultant relationship as it relates to creating a good impression. I have argued that the bodily experience of emotions is essential to understanding how the pressure to perform and manage the impression consultants make are both expressing power, politics, ethics, and individualising tendencies, patterns in the particular relations, and the identity of the consultant. I have described disappointment as an emotion that is particularly important to pay attention to within consultancy because it is related to clients' expectations about the performance of the consultant, and it might lead to the termination of contracts. Disappointment is important as an expression of the politics of the situation.

Fifth and last, I have contributed to the literature on organisational development with Ricoeur's notion of mutual recognition as an ethical approach. We always recognise others, even when we reject each other. The notion of mutual recognition means to recognise clients in ways in which we take clients seriously with curiosity and care. This offers a more nuanced perspective on what it means to help compared to the perspective on the consultant as it is often presented in the literature on organisational development (Clark & Avakian, 2013, p. 26). Mutual recognition of clients is more than positive affirmation because instrumental positive affirmation can be the exact opposite of mutual recognition. If affirmation is automated, it does not recognise the specific individual. The need for consultants to be flexible, adapt, and self-improve characterises much literature on organisational development. I am, with inspiration from Ricoeur, drawing attention to how self-constancy is vital to our sense of identity and to our capacity to act ethically and with care towards clients which might be in tension with the pressure to impress. Mutual recognition means to pay attention to one's own identity and intentions and recognise clients from this position. Taking others seriously, however, also means to listen to others and be prepared to change one's position. My contribution to knowledge is to draw attention to the paradoxical character of organisational development as it is about self-constancy (consultant's as well as client's) and identity-change at the same time. Processes of organisational change are about identity change for clients as well as for consultants.

Contribution to practice

I have taken up the themes of performance and impression management to contribute to the practice of consultancy within organisational development from my perspective as a self-employed consultant working primarily in public organisations in Denmark. I reflect on how my practice has changed and how this is relevant and recognisable to other consultants within organisational development.

The experience of going back to talk to Peter and John about what had happened between us is illustrative of the change I have experienced in my practice as a consultant. It marked a departure from the way I practiced consultancy and what would have been possible for me before I conducted this research. Anthropological and sociological research approaches have allowed me to 'think relationally', as Bourdieu phrases it (Bourdieu & Wacquant, 1992, p. 224), and gain detachment from my experienced need to impress. The change in my practice was due to the inquiry into emotions (taking my experiences and reactions seriously), power (paying attention to the politics of the situation), and ethics (taking others seriously with care and curiosity). The notion of mutual recognition has led me to take others seriously in ways where I am sharing my reactions, emotions, reflections, and convictions with honesty and courage to a higher degree than before I embarked on the DMan programme. I have described this approach in detail in both Projects 3 and 4.

This change of practice is not confined to the projects but characterises my practice more generally now. For example, I was invited to do a short presentation on an away-day for a larger group of managers recently. Several speakers were presenting, and the speaker immediately before me had provoked some disturbance among the participants. I felt it was important for the group to dwell on the disturbance and what it might mean for the group, so I suggested to the managers in charge of the event that I would explore this disturbance with the group instead of proceeding entirely with my planned presentation. They agreed, and we all found that the session offered a more productive way for the group to reflect upon themselves than my pre-planned presentation would have offered. The major difference from earlier was that I was detached to a degree where I could pay more attention to the process and not let the need to impress stand in the way of the needs of the group. The organisers of the event found that I was considerate of the group's needs as well as relaxed in a way that was helpful for them. I have gotten similar responses from my research colleagues in relation to the research we have been doing together. I experience myself less afraid of conflicts and keener to explore difference and what that might mean to me and clients. Research colleagues have expressed how I seem more relaxed and willing to engage in curious and honest exploration of critique and conflict, and how that feels less conflictual emotionally. I also experience that the responses I get from clients as I have been undertaking my work with this thesis are slightly different to earlier. Several have expressed that it feels comfortable to explore disagreements with me as a consultant. I agree, and I experience consultancy as a more honest space to engage and explore differences among us. Ironically, they are often more impressed with my interventions when I am trying less hard to impress.

Earlier, I would have feared that clients would not appreciate my opinions, that it would not be helpful or even inappropriate to take a position, and that I would not make an impression as competent. However, I often receive comments from clients about how it is relieving to engage in conversations about the experience of pressure to perform and impress and that I am legitimising discussion of disagreements, doubt, anxiety, and insecurities. I experience that these changes in my practice as a consultant enable me to help clients to inquire into what they are doing and why we are doing it in their work.

I have discussed my work with clients, and I have held three open workshops where I have presented my research with interested clients and colleagues. A smaller group has delved deeper, read my work, and discussed it with me. Everybody resonates with the experience of pressure to impress in consultancy, some with an intensity similar to mine, although I have realised that the experience is generally stronger for me compared to others. Similarly, others may not find themselves dependent on positive affirmation, as I have described. In that case, I hope they find it valuable to know how I (and other consultants who are like me in this regard) experience the pressure to perform to impress.

The research has enabled me to explore how the experienced need to impress affects consultancy. I have experienced a movement in my understanding of how performance, impression management, and politics work within the role of a consultant. The exploration of disappointment in Project 2 was a door opener for finding and exploring my research theme because understanding the relational character of emotions, under the influence of Burkitt (1999), allowed me to pay attention to what is going on in relationships. I have gradually gained a higher degree of detachment from my need to impress, which has allowed me to pay attention to power and ethics as a consultant. I have experienced a shift in my thinking where I am less occupied with whether others think positively about me and more occupied with whether their view of me might enable or constrain further conversation and what the wider consequences of my actions might be, for example, that the children in Projects 1 and 4 might have poorer service if I did not manage to speak up about ethics to the senior managers.

My practice has changed as I have been paying greater attention to the interdependency between people, and it has been helpful for me to think of myself as a researcher together with clients rather than trying to impress with an individual performance. For example, I recognise a pattern earlier where once I got a job, I tended to lose interest. The chase for the job seemed more important than the job itself, as if I chased for positive affirmation, and when I got it, I seemingly lost interest. The excitement of getting new jobs has changed in my practice as a consultant as I have worked with this thesis. I find myself engaging in more long-term relationships with clients where I am more dependent on others and feel less special, but also less isolated and lonely.

The research has helped me to describe my task as a consultant within organisational development as being about helping clients in their endeavours, caring for clients with curiosity, giving an account of myself, and exploring patterns of relating in ways that allow us to move on together. The exploration has been possible only through the engagement with the learning set and the wider DMan community. I have realised that I can explore who I am only with others. It is a contribution to the practice of consultancy that it is important to explore the impression I make on others as an ongoing process of inquiry. This is an exploratory mode and an ongoing practice that I will set up for myself with colleagues after my departure from the DMan community. In the following, I will describe movements in my practice that I have found recognisable more broadly for consultants within organisational development in Denmark.

First, understanding the relational character of emotions, from Burkitt (2012), has enabled discussions about what the experience of a need to impress and feelings of disappointment might express. I have found it relevant and valuable to bring emotions into conversations as 'data' or 'information'. This is not to suggest that our emotions have an objective character or that they are observable from a detached perspective, but to find a vocabulary that offers ways to discuss how we respond to the invitation to impress and how that affects our work together. It is a contribution to my practice that I am enabled to call into discussion how we are all trying to impress each other in different ways; how I am trying to come across as competent to the clients and how clients might feel a need to impress me, each other, managers, board members, key personnel, decision makers, etc.

Second, seeing consultants within organisational development as interdependent political agents with individual intentions has offered me a view of the inequality of the relation between consultants and clients. Consultants, on the one hand, are under pressure to perform and manage the impression they make in order to appear in control of future outcomes and the positive mindset of oneself, to be hired and continually remain professionally engaged. Whilst, on the other, they are expected to bring functional colluding, so-called negative emotions, patterns in relating that might be problematic, and one's own ethical convictions into conversation with clients. This entails, on rare occasions, when differences in ethical approaches render a continuation of the relation impossible, taking a stand and declining or rejecting further work together, as I described in the reflexive turn on Project 2. This requires the exercise of practical wisdom to take a position in politically savvy ways to allow all to move on together.

Third and last, mutual recognition as an ethics of care has offered ways to understand and discuss to a higher degree with clients everyone's intentions in relation to ethics, power, and identity. The ethics of mutual recognition implies self-constancy, so clients know the consultant. Voicing my position as a consultant might lead to disappointment, conflict, rejection, feelings of incompetence, and termination of contracts. However, detachment from the need to impress others and feeling less dependent on positive affirmation is enabling to care for others with curiosity in the spirit of mutual recognition.

Contribution to the wider practice of organisational development consultancy

The implications of my research could make a contribution to the wider practice of organisational development consultancy. In short, I am making a contribution to the practice of organisational development by showing how impression management is related to emotions, power, ethics and identity. I am making the point that there is a pressure for consultants to present themselves in certain ways to get and keep work and that it is impossible for consultants not to get caught up in trying to impress the client in certain ways. Consultants might be reluctant to contest and challenge customers in honest ways because consultants are dependent on clients to hire them. However, clients are also dependent on consultants as I described in Project 4. Consultants and clients are interdependent, and they are all involved in impressing each other. I am arguing that consultants are social actors with intentions of their own and that the practice of organisational development will benefit if consultant's ask questions of an anthropological and sociological nature to understand what is valued in the organisation and who benefits from their work. Paying attention to power offers a possibility to discuss different perspectives in ongoing conversations. The thesis reveals different scenarios around power negotiations as the loss of control, disappointment, and threats to identity. This stands in stark contrast to thinking of consultants as neutral facilitators, a view that dominates the descriptions of consultancy within organisational development. My research implies that consultants need to pay attention to their emotional reactions, doubts, insecurities and feelings of disappointment and share this with clients to some degree to enable the exploration of the politics of the situation. Consultants need to take many points of view into account and 'think relationally' as Bourdieu has coined it (1992). However, taking into account many points of view does not mean that consultants do not have views of their own. I am arguing that impressing others in ethical ways requires self-awareness and taking a position which means to enter the fluctuating paradox of constancy and change which can be very disturbing both for consultants and for the client. The alternative to reverberating to this paradox is to get lost in the other and therefore to lose oneself at the same time.

Conceiving the practice of consultancy within organisational development from the perspective of complex responsive processes of relating ascribes a central role to paradox more generally. The narratives in this thesis describe how consultancy driven by paradoxical tensions opposes the conceptualisations of consultants as neutral outsiders and consultancy as the practice of generic models. Pretending to be neutral and focusing on generic methods produces a lack of attention and mutual recognition. It is important to emphasise here that automated and instrumental positive affirmation can be the exact opposite of mutual recognition because it does not recognise the particular individual. Focusing on convincing and impressing clients (as in Project 2), implementing a project (as in Project 3), or navigating in power struggles (as in Project 4) distracted us from paying attention to what else was at stake. I am not saying, however, that generic models or positive affirmation of others should be avoided entirely. Generic models can be relevant as generalisations of past experiences and helpful to learn from experience. Just like positive affirmation of others can be both relevant, appropriate and well-earned. I call for consultants to notice and pay attention to what they do with clients while they are emotionally engaged in processes of organisational development together. As I argued with the help of Ricoeur (1992) in Project 4 we become aware of our habits and the ethics of the situation through experiencing a 'call' of consciousness. Being attentive to our state of mental unrest in these moments might enable us to become conscious about the politics and the ethics involved in the situation and offer opportunities to understand how our identity is at stake. I advocate that noticing emotional reactions and 'calls' of conscience, using this as data and sharing it with clients, is helpful for consultants and those they are working with to make sense of what is going on together

Further research

In this thesis, I have suggested that experiences of issues that *'imposes itself as obligation'* (Ricoeur, 1992, p. 170 italics in original) might be understood in the tradition of care ethics (Carney, 2015; Held, 2006) within organisational development. This work could be developed in an article with contributions to the understanding of care and recognition within organisational development from authors such as Logstrup (1997), Butler (2005), Arendt (1958), and Honneth (2003) in addition to Ricoeur (1992, 2005). I am particularly interested in developing and presenting the argument that an ethical practice entails that consultants be self-constant and take a position with clients. I find it important to explore how this might unfold within organisational development.

In the final stages of my work on this thesis I have continued my inquiries into the role of emotions within organisational development in a journal article. Two colleagues and I have been writing an article for the danish peer-reviewed journal "Kognition og indlæring" (English translation: "Cognition and learning") about emotions as data that are necessary to guide attention, discussions and decisions in processes of organisational development. The article has been accepted and is in press. I expect to continue to explore and write about emotions, power, ethics, and identity in the practice as a consultant within organisational development.

I have specific plans regarding my ongoing experimentation and development of the practice of consultancy within organisational development. I am planning to write a book with a colleague with whom I earlier authored a book. We both experience an obligation to participate in public debate to promote a view in which consultants are recognised as individuals with a specific history and identity. My wish is to contribute to a practice in which consultants describe, share, and explore disappointment and blame-games, rather than play them. I want to legitimise conversations about the pressure to impress and offer a vocabulary that challenges that of being a neutral professional with expert knowledge. I believe Ricoeur's ideas about ethics and narrative identity could be an important starting point in an ongoing exploration about how organisational development could be founded in mutual recognition that involves the consultant's positions, close relationships, friendship, and ethical convictions that inevitably lead to change in the identity of clients as well as consultants.

References

Alvesson, M., Skoldberg, K. (2018). *Reflexive Methodology* (Third). London: SAGE Publications Ltd.

Alvesson, M. (2001). Knowledge work: Ambiguity, image and identity. *Human Relations, 54*(7), 863–886.

Alvesson, M. (2009). At-Home Ethnography: Struggling with Closeness and Closure. In S. Ybema, D. Yanow, H. Wels, F. Kamsteeg, & M. Alvesson (Eds.), *Organizational Ethnography: Studying the Complexities of Everyday Life*. London: SAGE Publications Ltd.

Alvesson, M., & Billing, Y. D. (1997). *Understanding gender and organizations. Understanding Gender and Organizations*. London: Sage publications.

Alvesson, M., & Kärreman, D. (2011). *Qualitative Research and Theory Development*. London: SAGE Publications Ltd.

Alvesson, M., & Willmott, H. (2002). Identity regulation as organizational control: Producing the appropriate individual. *Journal of Management Studies, 39*(5), 619–644.

Alvesson, M., & Willmott, H. (2003). *Studying management critically. Studying Management Critically*. London: Sage Publications Ltd.

Andersen, T. (1987). The Reflecting Team: Dialogue and Meta-Dialogue in Clinical Work. *Family Process, 26*(4), 415–428.

Anderson, H., & Goolishian, H. (1992). The client is the expert: A not-knowing approach to therapy. In S. McNamee & K. J. Gergen (Eds.), *Therapy as social construction* (pp. 25–39). London: SAGE Publications Ltd.

Anderson, L. (2006). Analytic autoethnography. *Journal of Contemporary Ethnography*.

Arendt, H. (1958). *The human condition*. Chicago: The University of Chicago Press.

Argyris, C., Putnam, R., & McLain Smith, D. (1985). *Action Science: Concepts, Methods and Skills for Research and Intervention*. San Fransisco: Jossey-Bass Publishers.

Armstrong-Gibbs, F. (2019). On becoming an organizational autoethnographer. *Journal of Organizational Ethnography, 8*(2), 232–242.

Armstrong, M. (2009). *Armstrong's Handbook of Performance Management* (4th ed.). London: Kogan Page.

Ashdown, L. (2018). *Performance Management: A Practical Introduction*. London: Kogan Page.

Askeland, M. K. (2019). *Organisational Change and the Politics of Identity*. Doctoral Thesis University of Hertfordshire.

Asplund, J. (1972). *Om undren overfor samfundet (English: About curiosity towards society)*. Copenhagen: Hans Reitzels Forlag.

Baldwin, J. D. (1988). Habit, Emotion, and Self-Conscious Action. *Sociological Perspectives, 31*(1, January), 35–58.

Balkan, M. O., & Soran, S. (2013). The effects of impression management tactics on emotional expressions: Reseach on banking sector. *Journal of Global Strategic Management, 7*(1), 154–165.

Benschop, Y., van den Brink, M., Doorewaard, H., & Leenders, J. (2013). Discourses of ambition, gender and part-time work. *Human Relations, 66*(5), 699–723.

Bernstein, R. J. (1983). *Beyond objectivism and relativism: Science, Hermeneutics, and Praxis*. Philadelphia: University of Pennsylvania Press.

Bernstein, R. J. (1991). *The New Constellation: The Ethical-Political Horizons of Modernity/Postmodernity. Philosophy and Phenomenological Research*. United States of America: The MIT Press.

Bjørn, S. (2017). *Viklet ind i 1000 ting ting (english translation: Tangled up in 1000 things) on the album En ny fortælling begynder nu (English translation: A new tale is about to begin)*. Gateway Music.

Bolino, M. C., & Turnley, W. H. (1999). Measuring Impression Management in Organizations: A Scale Development Based on the Jones and Pittman Taxonomy. *Organizational Research Methods, 2*(2), 187–206.

Bourdieu, P. (1977). *Outline of a Theory of Practice*. Cambridge, UK: Cambridge University Press.

Bourdieu, P. (1990). *The Logic of Practice*. Stanford, California: Stanford University Press.

Bourdieu, P. (1991). *Language and Symbolic Power*. Cambridge, UK: Polity Press.

Bourdieu, P. (1994). De tre former for teoretisk viden (translated: "The three forms of theoretical knowledge"). In *Pierre Bourdieu: centrale tekster inden for sociologi og kulturteori*. København: Akademisk Forlag.

Bourdieu, P. (2005). *The social structures of the economy*. Cambridge, UK: Polity Press.

Bourdieu, P., & Wacquant, L. J. D. (1992). *An Invitation to Reflexive Sociology*. Cambridge, UK: Polity.

Bourgoin, A., & Harvey, J. F. (2018). Professional image under threat: Dealing with learning–credibility tension. *Human Relations, 71*(12), 1611–1639.

Brinkmann, S. (2012). *Qualitative Inquiry in Everyday Life - Working with Everyday*

Life Materials. London: Sage Publications Ltd.

Brinkmann, S. (2014). Doing Without Data. *Qualitative Inquiry, 20*(6), 720–725.

Brinkmann, S. (2017). *Stand Firm: Resisting the Self-Improvement Craze.* Cambridge: Polity Press.

Brinkmann, S. (2019). *The Joy of Missing Out: The Art of Self-Restraint in an Age of Excess*. Wiley.

Burkitt, I. (1999). *Bodies of Thought*. London: Sage publications.

Burkitt, I. (2012). Emotional Reflexivity: Feeling, Emotion and Imagination in Reflexive Dialogues. *Sociology, 46*(3), 458–472.

Bushe, G. (2010). *Clear Leadership*. Boston: Davies-Black.

Bushe, G. R., & Marshak, R. J. (2015). Dialogic Organization Development: The Theory and Practice of Transformational Change. In *Dialogic Organization Development: The Theory and Practice of Transformational Change*. Oakland: Berrett-Koehler.

Bushe, G. R., & Marshak, R. J. (2016). The Dialogic Organization Development Approach to Transformation and Change. In W. J. Rothwell, J. M. Stavros, & R. L. Sullivan (Eds.), *Practicing Organization Development: Leading Transformational Change: Fourth Edition* (4th ed.). San Fransisco: Wiley.

Butler, J. (2005). *Giving an account of oneself*. New York: Fordham University Press.

Cabanas, E., & Illouz, E. (2019). *Manufacturing Happy Citizens: How the Science and Industry of Happiness Control our Lives*. Cambridge, UK: Polity.

Campbell, D. (1995). *Learning Consultation: A Systemic Framework*. London: Karnac Books.

Carnegie, D. (2009). *How to Win Friends and Influence People*. New York: Simon & Schuster.

Carney, E. (2015). Depending on Practice: Paul Ricoeur and the Ethics of Care. *Les Ateliers de l'éthique, 10*(3).

Cecchin, G., Lane, G., & Ray, W. A. (2018). *Irreverence: A Strategy for Therapists' Survival. Systemic Thinking and Practice.* London: Routledge.

Clancy, A., Vince, R., & Gabriel, Y. (2012). That Unwanted Feeling: A Psychodynamic Study of Disappointment in Organizations. *British Journal of Management, 23*(4), 518–531.

Clark, T. (1995). *Managing consultants: Consultancy as the management of impressions.* London: Open University Press.

Clark, T., & Avakian, S. (2013). *Management consulting.* Cheltenham, England: Edward Elgar.

Clark, T., & Salaman, G. (1998). Creating the "right" impression: Towards a dramaturgy of management consultancy. *Service Industries Journal, 18*(1), 18–38.

Clegg, S. (2006). The bounds of rationality: Power/history/imagination. *Critical Perspectives on Accounting, 17*, 847–863.

Clegg, S., Carter, C., & Kornberger, M. (2004). 'Get up, I feel like being a strategy machine.' *European Management Review.*

Cooperrider, D. L. (2013). A contemporary commentary on Appreciative inquiry in organizational life. *Advances in Appreciative Inquiry, 4*, 3–67.

Cooperrider, D. L., & Srivastva, S. (1987). Appreciative Inquiry in Organizational life. *Resarch in Organizational Change and Develoment, 1*, 129–169.

Cunliffe, A. L., Luhman, J. T., & Boje, D. M. (2004). Narrative Temporality: Implications for Organizational Research. *Organization Studies, 25*(2), 261–286.

Curtis, G. (2018). *Functional Collusion in a UK Non Governmental Organisation:*

Processes of Shame and Exclusion from the Perspective of an Organisational Development Practitioner. Doctoral Thesis University of Hertfordshire.

Czarniawska, B. (1998). *A narrative approach to organization studies. Qualitative research methods* (Vol. 43). London: SAGE Publications Ltd.

Czarniawska, B., & Mazza, C. (2003). Consulting as a liminal space. *Human Relations, 56*(3), 267–290.

Delamont, S. (2007). Arguments against Auto-Ethnography. *Journal Of Contemporary Ethnography.*

Denison, D. R., Hooijberg, R., & Quinn, R. E. (1995). Paradox and Performance: Toward a Theory of Behavioral Complexity in Managerial Leadership. *Organization Science, 6*(5), 524–540.

Dewey, J. (1891). Moral Theory and Practice. *International Journal of Ethics, 1(2),* 186–203.

Dewey, J. (1910). *How we think.* Boston: D.C.Heath & Co.

Docheff, D. M. (1990). The Feedback Sandwich. *Journal of Physical Education, Recreation & Dance, 61*(9), 17–18.

Ehrenreich, B. (2010). *Smile or die.* London: Granta Publications.

Elias, N. (1978). *What is sociology?* New York: Columbia University Press.

Elias, N. (1986). *The loneliness of the dying.* Oxford: Basil Blackwell.

Elias, N. (2001). *The society of individuals.* New York: The Continuum International Publishing Group Inc.

Ellis, C. (2007). Telling Secrets, Revealing Lives: Relational Ethics in Research With Intimate Others. *Qualitative Inquiry, 13*(1), 3–29.

Emirbayer, M., & Johnson, V. (2008). Bourdieu and organizational analysis. *Theory and Society, 37*(1), 1–44.

Ericson, M., & Kjellander, B. (2018). The temporal becoming self—towards a Ricoeurian conceptualization of identity. *Scandinavian Journal of Management, 34*, 205–214.

Ferris, G. R., Treadway, D. C., Kolodinsky, R. W., Hochwarter, W. A., Kacmar, C. J., Douglas, C., & Frink, D. D. (2005). Development and validation of the political skill inventory. *Journal of Management, 31*(1), 126–152.

Fineman, S. (2006). On being positive: Concerns and counterpoints. *Academy of Management Review, 31*(2), 270–291.

Fineman, S., & Sturdy, A. (1999). The Emotions of Control: A Qualitative Exploration of Environmental Regulation. *Human Relations, 52*(5), 631–663.

Fitzgerald, S. P., Oliver, C., & Hoxsey, J. C. (2010). Appreciative inquiry as a shadow process. *Journal of Management Inquiry, 19*(3), 220–233.

Fleming, P., & Spicer, A. (2014). Power in Management and Organization Science. *Academy of Management Annals, 8*(1), 237–298.

French, W. L. & Bell, C. H. (1995). *Organisational development : Behavioural science interventions for organisational improvement* (Fifth). London: Prentice-Hall Inc.

Fuller, J. B., Barnett, T., Hester, K., Relyea, C., & Frey, L. (2007). An exploratory examination of voice behavior from a impression management perspective. *Journal of Managerial Issues, 19*(1), 134–151.

Gherardi, S. (2017). Unplugged - "Carte blanche." *Management (France), 20*(2), 208–220.

Gleitman, H. (1995). *Psychology* (4th ed.). Ww Norton & Co.

Goffman, E. (1959). *The Presentation of Self in Everyday Life.* Penguin Books, UK.

Goffman, E. (1967). *Interaction Ritual.* New York: Anchorbooks.

Gosovic, A. K. J. (2019). Gifts, reciprocity and ethically sound ethnographic research: a reflexive framework. *Journal of Organizational Ethnography, 9*(1), 66–79.

Greenblatt, S. (1997). The Touch Of The Real. *Representations, No. 59*(Summer), 14–29.

Han, B.-C. (2015). *The burnout society*. California: Stanford University Press.

Han, B.-C. (2019). *What Is Power?* Cambridge, UK: Polity Press.

Haslebo, G, Nielsen, K. (2000). Systems and Meaning: Consulting in Organizations.

Haslebo, G. (2004). *Relationer i Organisationer (English translation: Relations in Organisations)*. Copenhagen: Dansk Psykologisk Forlag.

Held, V. (2006). The Ethics Of Care. In D. Copp (Ed.), *The Oxford Handbook Of Ehitcal Theory*. New York: Oxford University Press.

Hochschild, A. R. (1979). Emotion Work, Feeling Rules, and Social Structure. *American Journal of Sociology, 85*(3), 551–575.

Hodgson, D. (2005). Putting on a professional performance: Performativity, subversion and project management. *Organization, 12*(1), 51–68.

Honneth, A. (2000). *Suffering from Indeterminacy. An Attempt at a Reactualization of Hegel's Philosophy of Right*. Assen: Van Gorcum & Comp.

Honneth, A. (2003). *Behovet for anerkendelse (English translation: "The need for recognition")*. Copenhagen: Hans Reitzels Forlag.

Honneth, A. (2006). *Kamp om anerkendelse (translated from "Kampf um Anerkennung: Zur moralischen Grammatik sozialer Konflikte")*. København: Hans Reitzels Forlag.

Ingold, T. (2018a). *Anthropology: Why it matters*. Cambridge, UK: Polity Press.

Ingold, T. (2018b). *Anthropology and/as education*. Oxon: Routledge.

Joas, H., & Knöbl, W. (2009). *Social theory: Twenty introductory lectures. Social Theory: Twenty Introductory Lectures* (5th ed.). New York: Cambridge University Press.

John, O. P., Robins, R. W., & Pervin, L. A. (1999). *Handbook of Personality: Theory and Research. Handbook of personality Theory and research* (Vol. 2).

Josselson, R. (2004). The hermeneutics of faith and the hermeneutics of suspicion. *Narrative Inquiry, 14*(1), 1–28.

Kemp, P. (2002). Narrative ethics and moral law in Ricoeur. In J. Wall, W. Schweiker, & D. Hall (Eds.), *Paul Ricoeur and contemporary moral thought*. London: Routledge.

Kristensen, J. G. (2006). *Den selvopfyldende profeti der tryllebinder HR (english translation: The selffulfilling prophecy that charms HR)*. Doctoral Thesis Copenhagen University.

Larsen, H., & Friis, P. (2017). Improvising in Research: Drawing on Theatre Practices. In *Collaborative Research Design*. Singapore: Springer Verlag.

Larsen, S. B., & Gregersen, J. (2017). *At lede efter kompleksitet (English translation: Searching for complexity)*. Forlaget Mindspace.

Latour, B. (1996). *Aramis - or the love of technology*. Massachusetts: Harvard University Press.

Logstrup, K. E. (1997). *Ethical demand*. London: University of Notre Dame Press.

Lukes, S. (2005). *Power: A Radical View* (Second Edi). Hampshire: Palgrave Macmillan.

Lüscher, L. (2012). *Ledelse gennem paradokset (english translation: Leadership by paradox)*. Copenhagen: Dansk Psykologisk Forlag.

Mallett, O., & Wapshott, R. (2012). Mediating ambiguity: Narrative identity and knowledge workers. *Scandinavian Journal of Management, 28*(1), 16–26.

Martela, F. (2015). Fallible Inquiry with Ethical Ends-in-View: A Pragmatist Philosophy of Science for Organizational Research. *Organization Studies, 36*(4), 537–563.

Maxton, P. J., & Bushe, G. R. (2018). Individual Cognitive Effort and Cognitive Transition During Organization Development. *Journal of Applied Behavioral Science, 54*(4), 424–456.

Mead, G.H. (1932). *The philosophy of the present*. London: The Open Court Company.

Mead, G.H. (1934). *Mind, Self, and Society*. London: The University of Chicago Press Ltd.

Mead, Geore Herbert. (1934). *Mind, Self & Society*. Chicago: The University of Chicago Press.

Mead, George Herbert. (1925). The Genesis of the Self and Social Control. *The International Journal of Ethics, 35*(3), 251–277.

Méndez, M. G. (2013). Autoethnography as a research method: Advantages, limitations and criticisms. *Colombian Applied Linguistics Journal, 15*(2), 279–287.

Messner, M., Clegg, S., & Kornberger, M. (2008). Critical Practices in Organizations. *Journal of Management Inquiry2, 17*(2), 68–82.

Michel, J. (2015). *Ricoeur and the post-structuralists*. London: Rowman & Littlefield Internation, Ltd.

Mowles, Chris. (2009). Consultancy as temporary leadership: negotiating power in everyday practice -. *International Journal of Learning and Change, 3*(2009), 281–293.

Mowles, Chris. (2015). *Managing in uncertainty: Complexity and the paradoxes of everyday organizational life*. London: Routledge.

Mowles, Chris. (2017). Group Analytic Methods Beyond the Clinical Setting—Working with Researcher–Managers. *Group Analysis, 50*(2), 217–236.

Mowles, Christopher. (2011). *Rethinking Management - Radical Insights from the Complexity Sciences*. Surrey: Ashgate Publishing Group.

Norman, K. (2012). A uniform experience? Reflections on implementing rules into practice. *International Journal of Leadership in Public Services, 8*(4), 191–200.

Nussbaum, M. (2002). Ricoeur on tragedy. In J. Wall, W. Schweiker, & D. Hall (Eds.), *Paul Ricoeur and contemporary moral thought*. london: Routledge.

Pardales, M. J., & Girod, M. (2006). Community of Inquiry: Its past and present future. *Educational Philosophy and Theory, 38*(3), 299–309.

Pellauer, D. (2007). *Ricoeur. A guide for the perplexed*. London: Continuum International Publishing Group.

Reed, M. I. (2001). Organization, trust and control: A realist analysis. *Organization Studies*.

Ricoeur, P. (1992). *Oneself as Another*. Chicago: The University of Chicago Press.

Ricoeur, P. (2005). *The Course of Recognition*. Cambridge, Massachusetts: Harvard University Press.

Roberts, L. M. (2005). Changing faces: Professional image construction in diverse organizational settings. *Academy of Management Review, 30*(4), 685–711.

Rosenfeld, P. (1997). Impression management, fairness, and the employment interview. *Journal of Business Ethics, 16*(8), 801–808.

Rosenfeld, P., Giacalone, R., & Riordan, C. A. (1995). *Impression Management in Organizations: Theory, Measurement, Practice*. London: Routledge.

Runciman, D. (2018). *Political hypocrisy: the mask of power, from Hobbes to Orwell and beyond* (2nd ed.). New Jersey: Princeton University Press.

Sandberg, J., & Tsoukas, H. (2011). Grasping the logic of practice: Theorizing through practical rationality. *Academy of Management Review, 36*(3), 338–360.

Scharff, C. (2015). Blowing your own trumpet: Exploring the gendered dynamics of self-promotion in the classical music profession. *Sociological Review, 63*(S1), 97–112.

Schein, E. (1987). *Process consultation, Vol. II: Lessons for Managers and Consultants.* (Addison-Wesley, Ed.), *Cambridge:Addison-Wesley Publishing Company* (Second). Reading, Massachusets.

Schein, E. (1999). *Process consultation revisited: Building the helping relationship.* Reading, Massachusets: Addison-Wesley.

Schein, E. (2017). *Organizational Culture and Leadership Organizational Culture and Leadership. Wiley & Sons, Inc.* (Fifth). Hoboken, New Jersey: Wiley & Sons, Inc.

Schein, E. H. (1995). Process consultation, action research and clinical inquiry: Are they the same? *Journal of Managerial Psychology, 10*(6), 14–19.

Schein, E. H. (2006). From brainwashing to organizational therapy. *Organization Studies, 27*(2), 287–301.

Schnoor, M., & Jack, M. (2020). *Den Interne Konsulent (English translation: The Internal Consultant).* Copenhagen: Dansk Psykologisk Forlag.

Senge, P. (1990). The fifth discipline. *The Art & Practice of Learning Organization.*

Sennett, R. (1998). *The Corrosion of Character.* New York: Ww Norton & Co.

Sennett, R. (2007). *The Culture of the New Capitalism.* Yale University Press.

Shaw, P. (1997). Intervening in the shadow systems of organizations. *Journal of Organizational Change Management, 10*(3), 235–250.

Shaw, P. (2002). *Changing conversations in organizations : a complexity approach to change*. London: Routledge.

Shields, P. M. (2003). The community of inquiry: Classical Pragmatism and Public Administration. *Administration and Society, 35*(5), 510–538.

Smith, D., & Katzenbach, J. (1994). *The wisdom of teams: Creating the high-performance organization*. New York: HarperCollins Publishers Inc.

Smith, I. S. (2008). *Management consulting in action*. Doctoral Thesis Copenhagen Business School.

Snowden, D. (2005). Strategy in the context of uncertainty. *Handbook of Business Strategy, 6*(1), 47–54.

Solso, K. (2016). *The Covering of Power and Politics in Everyday Management Practice*. Doctoral Thesis University of Hertfordshire.

Sparrowe, R. T. (2005). Authentic leadership and the narrative self. *Leadership Quarterly, 16*, 419–439.

Spradley, J. (1979). *The Ethnographic Interview*. Orlando: Harcourt Brace Jovanovich College Publishers.

Stacey, R., & Mowles, C. (2016). *Strategic Management and Organisational Dynamics* (Seventh). Harlow: Pearson Education Limited.

Stacey, R. (2001). *Complex Responsive Processes in Organizations. Complex Responsive Processes in Organizations*. London: Routledge.

Stacey, R. D. (2003). *Complexity and group processes: A radically social understanding of individuals*. Oxfordshire: Routledge.

Stacey, R. D. (2012). *Tools and techniques of leadership and management: Meeting the challenge of complexity*. London: Routledge.

Stacey, R., & Griffin, D. (2005). *A complexity perspective on researching organizations*. (R. Stacey & D. Griffin, Eds.). Oxon: Routledge.

Stein, F. (2017). *Work, sleep, repeat: the abstract labour of German management consultants*. London: Bloomsbury Academic.

Stein, F. (2018a). Boundary work – power and liminality in management consulting. In K. Olaf, J. Heilbron, F. Bühlmann, & M. Savage (Eds.), *New Directions in Elite Studies* (pp. 280–296). London: Routledge.

Stein, F. (2018b). Selling Speed: Management Consultants, Acceleration, and Temporal Angst. *Political and Legal Anthropology Review, 41*(S1), 103–117.

Stoltz, H. T. (2020). *Processes of Compromise in International Development Consultancies—Getting Heard as a Social Scientist*. Doctoral Thesis University of Hertfordshire.

Streatfield, P. (2001). *The Paradox of Control in Organizations*. London: Routledge.

Sturdy, A. (1997). The Consultancy Process - An Insecure Business? *Journal of Management Studies, 34*(3), 389–413.

Sturdy, A., Schwarz, M., & Spicer, A. (2006). Guess who's coming to dinner? Structures and uses of liminality in strategic management consultancy. *Human Relations, 59*(7), 929–960.

Sullivan, S. (2000). Reconfiguring Gender with John Dewey: Habit, Bodies, and Cultural Change. *Hypatia, 15*(1), 22–42.

Taylor, C. (1991). *The Ethics of Authenticity*. Cambridge: Harvard University Press.

Venema, H. I. (2000). *Identifying Selfhood: Imagination, Narrative, and Hermeneutics in the Thought of Paul Ricoeur*. New York: State University of New York Press.

Vince, R., & Gabriel, Y. (2011). Organizations, Learning and Emotions. In *Handbook of Organizational Learning & Knowledge Management* (pp. 331–348).

Vine, T. (2020). Brexit, Trumpism and paradox: Epistemological lessons for the critical consensus. *Organization, 27*(3), 466–487.

Vine, T., Clark, J., Richards, S., & Weir, D. (2018). *Ethnographic research and analysis: Anxiety, identity and self. Ethnographic Research and Analysis: Anxiety, Identity and Self*. London: Palgrave Macmillan.

Wallace, M. (2002). The summoned self. In J. Wall, W. Schweiker, & D. Hall (Eds.), *Paul Ricoeur and contemporary moral thought*. London: Routledge.

Watzlawick, P., Weakland, J., & Fisch, R. (1974). *Change: Principles of problem formation and problem resolution*. New York: Ww Norton & Co.

Weiss, B., & Feldman, R. S. (2006). Looking good and lying to do it: Deception as an impression management strategy in job interviews. *Journal of Applied Social Psychology, 36*(4), 1070–1086.

Wetherell, M. (2012). *Affect and emotion*. London: Sage publications.

Wheatley, M., & Frieze, D. (2011). Leadership in the Age of Complexity : From Hero to Host. *Resurgence Magazine*.